Investing in You:
Using The Power of Positive Thinking

Table of Contents

INTRODUCTION..5
    Positive Thinking is a Bunch of Crap – and Crap Makes Great Fertilizer....................5
PLANTING YOUR SEEDS...9
    Roots: What's In Your Garden Now?...11
    Self-Esteem: Catching the I-Love-Me Disease..11
    Me-ology: The Self-Esteem Dipstick...13
    The Dark Ages: Childhood Programming and Past Letdowns..................................24
    Exercise: Connect-the-influences..26
    Getting Back on the Horse..28
    Step Away from the Panic Button: Conquering Fear..30
    Trauma: Breaking the Chains...36
    "It Could Be Worse": Dramatization and Awareness..38
    For Your Eyes Only: Journaling to Release..40
    Meditation: Connecting Above Pain...45
    Join the Club: Live and Online Support Groups..49
    Drop That Horseshoe: There's No Such Thing as Bad Luck....................................51
    Change Your Mind, Change Your Life...53
    Warm-up: Shake Out Negative Kinks..55
    Work Those Mouth Muscles..56
    Do Some Reps..58
    Cool-Down: Feel the Burn...60
    Switching Terminals: Hook Up to Positive Energy...62
    What's In It for Me?...63
    The Buddy System...65

    Knowledge is Power..65

    Sign on the Dotted Line...69

    Dangle Your Own Carrot...70

    Surrender...72

SHOOTS AND LEAVES..74

    The First Signs of Your Spring of Rebirth..75

    Conspiracy Theory: The Biggest Threat to the New You.......................................77

    There"s Always Tomorrow: Eradicate Procrastination..78

    Just Say No: How Not to Take On Too Much..81

    Take Me As I Am: Kicking the Approval Habit...87

    Know Your Code...88

    Graduate from High School...89

    Weed Your Friendship Garden..91

    Blood is Thicker than Embarrassment..92

    The Blame Game: Whose Fault Is It, Anyway?...95

    Making Your Omelet: How to Learn From Your Mistakes....................................96

    Give Yourself Permission...97

    Make Interesting Mistakes..98

    „Fess Up...99

    Pinpoint Your Error...100

    Talk About It..101

    Keep Good Records...102

    If Your Buds Shrivel, Add More Fertilizer...104

    When the Door Closes, Go Out the Window...105

    Buried Alive: What to Do When Your Mountain Crumbles................................107

    Using Your Lifelines...108

OPENING YOUR BLOSSOMS..111

    Poppy Fields: Visualizing in Technicolor...111

    Preparation: Boarding the Visualization Train..113

    Preparation: Boarding the Visualization Train..111
    Guided visualization...114
    Receptive visualization...116
    Altered memory visualization..118
    Worry-Me-Nots and You-Can-Themums...121
    Cross-Pollination: How to "Bee"..125

FRUITION AND HARVEST..140
    Natural Attraction: Bringing Love, Money and Success............................142
    Radiant Relationships...143
    Incredible Careers...146
    Financial Freedom...150
    Dream Delivery..152
    Awesome Aging..153

THE PHYSICAL POWER OF POSITIVE THINKING............................155
    Sit Back and Relax..158

CONCLUSION...163
    Surviving the Winter: Keep Your Garden Alive....................................163

CHECKLIST FOR THE POSITIVE THINKING PROCESS....................165
BIBLIOGRAPHY..166

INTRODUCTION

Positive Thinking is a Bunch of Crap – and Crap Makes Great Fertilizer

"A positive attitude may not solve all your problems, but it will annoy enough people to make it worth the effort."
Herm Albright

At some point in your life, you've probably heard about the power of positive thinking. Basically, this is a theory that contends if you believe good things will happen to you, there will be some sort of cataclysmic shift in the energies surrounding you which will actually *cause good things to happen to you*. For as many people who believe in the power of positive thinking, there are many more who believe it's all a bunch of New Age pop psychology drivel or sugar-coated Peter Pan platitudes.

Here's the kicker: they're all right.

You see, positive thinking is a system of beliefs. So if you believe it doesn't work- then, of course, it won't work. And if you believe it *does* work...well, you get the idea. For non-believers, using positive thinking is like trying to get a job after high school. You need experience to get a job, but you need a job to get the experience. It can be difficult to know where you"re supposed to start. But just like any other process, the key to making positive thinking work for you is to start small. Plant seeds, if you will, and then learn how to tend and cultivate those seeds until you have a mental garden that bears a phenomenal crop, year after year. Anything is possible with positive thinking...even if you do believe it"s all a bunch of crap.

Norman Vincent Peale, the father of positive thinking, once said: "If you have zest and enthusiasm you attract zest and enthusiasm. Life does give back in kind." This is the essence of positive thinking. It"s not so much a theory as it is a contagious disease. Just as anger and negativity spread quickly from person to person, so do humor and happiness- only good feelings spread far faster. Think about it: have you ever noticed that the quickest way to ease a tense situation is to make a joke? The instant someone laughs or smiles, a sense of relief spreads through everyone in the vicinity. Even if the angered parties don"t feel better, they are at least able to discuss the problem in a detached and objective way, and get on with their lives instead of dwelling on negativity. For that same reason, solo drivers who get cut off in traffic tend to remain angry for at least the rest of the drive-because there is no one else near them to send out good vibrations and break the tension. Makes sense, doesn't it?

If you've picked up this book and read this far, the seeds of belief are already there. Your next step is to clear your mind's garden of doubt and get ready to plant. You'll learn how to take all that negativity and mulch it down into fertilizer that will let your possibilities grow.

Now grab your shovel, and let's head in to the garden.

The biggest tree in the world grows from a seed you can hold between two fingers.

"Whether you think you can or whether you think you can't...you're right."
- Henry Ford

PLANTING YOUR SEEDS

"In every phenomenon the beginning remains always the most notable moment."
- Thomas Carlyle

To tune in to the power of positive thinking, you should probably start small- particularly if you don"t believe it will work. It"s one thing to tell yourself, "Tomorrow, when I wake up in the morning I won"t hit snooze a dozen times and feel drowsy for the rest of the day," and quite another to tell yourself, "Tomorrow, when I wake up in the morning I"ll be living independently wealthy and living in a mansion." (Unless, of course, you are in fact independently wealthy and living in a mansion at the moment; in which case you might try to think your way into ownership of a small country.)

The process of making positive thinking work for you begins with destruction, or at least a mild shift in your thought structure. In order to make room for new methods and ideas, you must first tear out all the old negativity patterns you"ve been building throughout your life. For some, this can be a gradual process: as you witness positive thinking work for you, one small step at a time, you will slowly clear out those good-things-only-happen-to-other-people thoughts, and be able to cultivate the seeds of change.

Roots: What's In Your Garden Now?

"The greatest revolution of our generation is the discovery that human beings, by changing the inner attitudes of their minds, can change the outer aspects of their lives."
- William James

What"s holding you back? Even those who fully embrace the theory of positive thinking may feel some qualms over entrusting their lives to mere thought. There are many possibilities that could be producing weeds in your mental garden, and the best way to get rid of a weed is to yank it out, roots and all. In this section we'll discuss some of the most common stumbling blocks people encounter on the road to positive thinking, as well as how to overcome them and lay the foundation for a healthy life outlook.

Self-Esteem: Catching the I-Love-Me Disease

For most of human existence, self-esteem was an unheard-of notion akin to the theories of those heretics who believed the world was round. The term "self-esteem" - defined by Webster"s Dictionary as "pride in oneself; self-respect" - made its way into the common public awareness during the „60s and „70s as a catch-all term to describe the essence of parenting problems. The "old ways" of parenting were pronounced barbaric and damaging to the budding self-esteem of our youth, and many parents fearful of raising unhappy, ill-adjusted children took advice that led to a generation of children with high self-esteem...so high it eclipsed personal responsibility and created a "me-first" mentality.

On the other hand, most of us are taught that thinking highly of ourselves is a vain, selfish and undesirable trait. Advice telling us to feel better about ourselves and occasionally put us first seems counterintuitive at best. After all, isn"t self-love the first step on the road to Ego Central? Many people want to feel good about themselves, but guilt too often rears its ugly head and stops healthy self-esteem from developing.

Because of these conflicting viewpoints, self-esteem is a tricky little emotion to manipulate. It"s important to strike a balance between modesty and greed. It takes practice to convince yourself that you are a worthwhile and deserving person, while at the same time keeping in mind that you"re not the center of the universe. Though it may sound impossible, it"s actually simple to accomplish.

Where do you rate on the self-esteem-o-meter? The following quiz will help you gauge your feelings and identify areas that need improvement.

Me-ology: The Self-Esteem Dipstick

To rate your self-esteem, choose the answer that most closely reflects your likely reaction to the following situations:

1. You know you're good at creating databases. Your boss asks you and several co-workers for a volunteer to organize a new client information database, and another volunteer to write a company newsletter- which you have no idea how to do. You:

    A. Volunteer for both, because you're so brilliant you'll be able to figure it out - even at the expense of embarrassing the company the first few times you write a terrible newsletter.

    B. Volunteer for the database- and when Fred Jones also volunteers, gently point out that you"ve had more experience, but would be happy to teach him what you know as you go along.

C. Remain silent. Someone else is surely better at it than you, and the boss would never pick you anyway.

2. You're out with friends and you've just passed gas noisily in the middle of a restaurant, so you:

A. Immediately blame a passing waiter or someone else at your table. You are completely serious in your accusations, and there"s no way anyone will be able to pin it on you. If they even think about it, you'll let them have it.

B. Crack a joke about that four-bean salad you had for lunch.

C. Attempt to crawl under the table, then excuse yourself and head to the bathroom. You can't face any of them for the rest of the night, and you consider paying the entire check right now and leaving before they notice you're gone- *if* they notice you"re gone.

3. When you watch Jeopardy or play Trivial Pursuit, you:

A. Laugh at the other players when they get the answers wrong. You know them all, and if you ever went on Jeopardy you"d clean them out.

B. Have a blast. You know some of the answers and try to guess at the rest. You love to learn new things.

C. Don't watch Jeopardy or play Trivial Pursuit. You're not smart enough for stuff like that.

4. You've decided to go after that promotion at work. You:

A. Make a bunch of other people look bad so there's no way you'll be passed up.

B. Let your boss know you're interested in the promotion, and then put in some extra effort to prove you're good for the position.

C. Decide on the drive to work that you're not going to go for it after all. You won't get it no matter what you do, so there's no point in trying.

5. When making a tough decision, you:

A. Choose the option that sounds best for you at the moment, and then stick to your decision no matter what, even if it turns out to be the wrong one.

B. Weigh your options and think about the advantages and disadvantages of each one before deciding on your final choice, but remain open to change if it turns out there is a better way.

C. Decisions? You can't make decisions. You always pick the wrong thing and wind up making everyone miserable. You'll get someone else to decide.

6. *You're faced with an entire evening alone. You:*

A. Gloat, because you don't have to spend time in the company of those miserable cretins who think they're your friends, but can't hold a candle to your brilliant and sparkling personality. You know they"re all sitting around wishing they could hang with you, anyway.

B. Take the time to do something you enjoy, like take a long bath, read a good book, or fix yourself your favorite dinner. It"s nice to relax once in a while and be alone with your thoughts.

C. Resign yourself to being miserable all night. You might as well go to bed early and hope someone"s around tomorrow.

7. *When performing a task that requires your full concentration, you:*

A. Don"t. Whatever it is you"re doing, you could do it in your sleep. You don't have to bother concentrating on things.

B. Are able to tune out most distractions and complete the task to the best of your ability. You are determined to put your best foot forward.

C. Can"t. You"re too nervous about screwing things up to concentrate, so you tend to work on projects in short bursts and often end up finishing things late because you"re so distracted.

8. A friend introduces you to someone new. You:

A. Prove that you"re a better person by saying something witty or clever that lets them know your friend is paying attention to you right now, not them. If the new person is worth knowing, they'll make the effort to get to know you.

B. Greet him or her warmly, introduce yourself and ask an open-ended question such as "What do you do for a living?" or "Where do you live?" You"re prepared to actually listen to the answer and will reserve judgment until you get to know the person better.

C. Mumble "hello," and then slink off in search of a friend who"s not talking to someone you don"t know. Whoever the new person is,

they wouldn"t want to get to know you anyway.

9. You walk in to your house and you're greeted by an awful stench: the refrigerator is unplugged, and everything in it is spoiled. You:

A. Immediately assume someone was screwing around with it and launch an investigation to find the culprit.

B. First plug it back in to find out if it still works, and then try to figure out what happened. If someone else was responsible for unplugging it, they can help you clean it out. In any case, you'll do what"s necessary to correct the problem.

C. Decide you must have done something wrong, and now it"s coming back to haunt you. You grumble under your breath as you clean out the refrigerator and wonder why things like this always have to happen to you.

10. Your supervisor calls you into the office to compliment you on the tremendous job you're doing on your new project. You:

A. Thank him outwardly, all the while thinking it"s about time he noticed how great you are. Maybe now you'll get the respect you deserve.

B. Are sincerely flattered, and tell him so. You also ask if there is anything you could be doing better.

C. Insist that you"re not really doing all that well, and try to hurry him along so you can escape. You don"t deserve praise.

11. You have to talk to your boss about a recent event that is affecting the way you and your co-workers perform your job. You:

A. Act as though you and your boss are best buddies, and demand that she do something to fix the problem. After all, you could be running the show just as easily as her, and you"d probably do a better job.

B. Approach the matter professionally and with confidence that a solution can be found. You offer any suggestions you might have to correct the problem, and ask if she has any ideas about what should be done.

C. Would never presume to talk to your boss. There"s a reason she is the boss and you"re not. You might send her an anonymous e-mail or ask one of your co-workers to talk to her.

12. This weekend you have a hundred little projects at home that have to be tackled, and you're feeling a bit overwhelmed. You:

    A. Attack several things at once, starting with the easiest ones. You might not manage to finish any of them, but you can always insist that someone else pitch in, because you have more important things to do.

    B. Decide which projects need to be completed first and take them on one at a time. By taking things step by step, you will finish what needs to be done. If anyone else is available at home, you'll ask them to help out.

    C. Bemoan the unfortunate twist of fate that ruined your weekend. There"s no way you'll ever be able to finish everything. You don"t ask anyone else for help because they have better things to do than perform favors for you, and you wouldn"t want to be a bother.

13. The opportunity arises for you to pursue your dream job, but it would mean leaving your current, stable position right away. You:

    A. Drop everything and go for it. Who needs a safety net?

B. Weigh your options, and plan out what you'll do if the new opportunity falls through. If you have a spouse, you discuss the decision with them and create a backup plan. If it's possible, you'll find a way to make it work.

C. Stay right where you are. Why risk disappointment? You just know it won't work out.

14. You have five minutes to get to an appointment, and you're stuck in a seemingly endless traffic jam at a dead stop. You:

A. Curse, fume, and honk your horn repeatedly. Don't these people realize you"re in a hurry?

B. Are frustrated, but you know there isn't much you can do change the situation. If you have a cell phone, you call to let them know you"re going to be a little late. You use the unexpected time to relax and listen to your favorite radio station, or just to think.

C. Want to die. Things like this always seem to happen to you. It just isn't fair. You're so worried about being late you're feeling sick, and there"s no way you'll be able to relax until you're out of this mess.

15. A co-worker reviews one of your projects and tells you a few things that aren't pleasant, but they are valid points. You:

A. Thank him through clenched teeth, but insist that you know what you"re doing. He has a lot of nerve criticizing your work, and his opinions don"t really matter anyway.

B. Are grateful for the opportunity to improve your work. You thank him for his insight and go back over the project with his suggestions in mind before turning it in.

C. Give up. You can"t do anything right. Maybe your co-worker should have been in charge of this project instead of you. You"ll just turn it in and hope you don"t get fired for incompetence.

Gloomy Gus?

Results: Tally up all your A, B, and C answers to find out where you rate on the self-esteem dipstick:

Mostly A:

Put Down That Mirror, Narcissus. Your tank overfloweth. You may not be aware of it, but you have far more confidence than you need. While confidence is a good trait to possess, too much of it can make you appear arrogant, rude or unapproachable. Try to take more notice of others" feelings, and you'll get much further.

Or tenacious flower?

Mostly B:

Join the Circus, You Have Perfect Balance. You have a healthy level of self-esteem tempered with empathy and concern for others. You're probably the life of the party or the person everyone comes to for help, and you're glad to give it when you can- but you know when you need time for yourself.

Mostly C:

If You Dig Any Deeper You'll End Up in China. You're a few quarts low, and you could use a self-esteem top-off. You may think you can't do anything right, but with a little confidence and some positive

thinking, you'll find you are worth far more than you believe. If you answered C to everything, it's time for a complete system flush and refill.

The Dark Ages: Childhood Programming and Past Letdowns

> *"Upon our children, how they are taught, rests the fate- or fortune- of tomorrow's world."*
> *- B. C. Forbes*

The things we learn in childhood aren't easy to forget- mostly because we don't actively remember them. It is far harder to dislodge subconscious thought. When we are unaware not only of *why* we embrace or avoid certain things, but also unaware of the fact that we *are* embracing or avoiding them, pinpointing the roots of our actions is a difficult process.

Childhood lessons don't always come from our parents, and often not even the messages we received from them were intentionally placed there. For example, if you parents raised you to be helpful, courteous, polite, and giving, you may have learned those lessons so well that the very idea of doing something for yourself makes you cringe- and you may not know why. On the other hand, if your parents gave you everything you wanted without you ever asking for it or lifting a finger, you may project those same expectations on everyone around you- again, with no idea why you"re doing it, or even that you are doing it at all. Many times, outwardly selfish people are shocked to discover that others perceive them as selfish. They may even believe themselves the kindest, most benevolent people they know.

Another factor you may not consider when trying to access your childhood programming is the outside influences that affected your formation. Teachers, daycare workers or babysitters, school friends, even random adults in the grocery store may have had an impact on your behaviors and beliefs, whether consciously or unconsciously.

Though it may be impossible to determine all of your childhood influences, you can give yourself a general idea of past events and personalities that shaped your current beliefs and take steps to change them. The following brief exercise will help you get started thinking about your triggers and habits.

Exercise: Connect-the-influences

1. Starting with your parents, list the names of every person you can recall that you associated with during childhood in a single column down the left-hand side of a sheet of paper. If you don't know the name of a person, use a brief description such as "the lady at the end of the street with the loud little dog." Include family, friends, teachers, caregivers, neighbors, and anyone else you remember. If you run out of room, tape another piece of paper to the bottom of the first one and keep going down the left-hand side.

2. On the right-hand side of the paper, list all the habits and traits you possess, both good and bad. If you're feeling brave, ask a friend to help you come up with some of the traits you possess that you might not be aware of. You don't even have to show anyone your list; you can call them up and tell them you're getting a head start on your New Year's resolutions.

3. Now comes the fun part. Try to match each habit or trait with one of the people from the left-hand column, and draw a line to connect them. You may find that some people have several connecting lines, while others have none. Pay close attention to the people who seem to have appeared on your list for no particular reason. If you remember them clearly, they probably influenced your life in some small way.

This exercise is not meant to lay blame on the people in your past for ruining your life. Rather, it is to illustrate that many of your flaws and negative qualities are a result of things you learned as an impressionable child, and therefore can be let go of without guilt. Children see things through a different lens than adults do, and what we learn at an early age can often end up coloring everything we do as grownups. Fortunately, we can learn to let go of those negative tendencies once we view them with the wisdom and rationality we have developed along the way.

Getting Back on the Horse

> *"If you have made mistakes, even serious ones, there is always another chance for you. What we call failure is not the falling down, but the staying down."*
> *- Mary Pickford*

Beyond childhood, you may have experienced setbacks or letdowns for which you clearly recall the reasoning. Often we are so opposed to change that the slightest sign a new way of doing things isn't working out becomes the signal to stop trying. We are creatures of habit, and breaking the mold we"ve created for ourselves is a challenge few feel they have the time or the energy to face.

Fortunately, we can chip away at that mold until the cracks become wide enough to break free. According to most psychologists, it takes 21 days to break a habit. The actions and reactions you develop in response to letdowns are nothing more than habits that you can rid yourself of with practice.

Your own thinking may be "fencing you in"!

Ready for another exercise? Make a list of all the things you"ve tried and stopped doing before completing (remember, you haven"t failed at them- you have simply made a temporary pit stop on the path to success). This list might include diets, resolutions, exercise habits, quitting smoking, or even self-help programs like this one. Leave yourself some space after each item. When you get to the end of the list, go back and fill in those habits you have developed as a consequence of waiting to follow through. For example, if you listed "The Atkins Diet," your habit might be "overindulging on pasta because I didn't eat any for six months." Some of your habits may be simple to change; others may require deviation from your intended course. In the pasta example, you might realize you can still eat pasta, just not as often as you have been while making up for the loss. Come up with an alternative for each habit that you can live with, so you don't short yourself before you get started. You might decide to have pasta twice a week instead of every other night.

Now that you have a guide, you can start implementing successful changes one step at a time. Choose one or two habits you"d like to change, and be sure to implement the changes daily for 21 days in a row. It"s helpful to keep a journal or a chart to remind yourself what you"re working on and why. You can also treat yourself to a reward after the successful completion of each habit-breaking cycle. How about a nice, big plate of spaghetti? Go ahead; you"ve earned it!

Step Away from the Panic Button: Conquering Fear

"All of us are born with a set of instinctive fears- of falling, of the dark, of lobsters, of falling on lobsters in the dark or speaking before the Rotary Club, and of the words "Some Assembly Required."
- Dave Barry

Where all else fails to stop us from achieving what we want from life, fear steps in. We experience fear on both conscious and unconscious levels, and it is one of the most limiting emotions we possess. In some cases fear is justified, and even healthy. For example, a person contemplating crossing a busy street will harbor a healthy fear of being struck by two tons of rapidly moving steel commonly known as a motor vehicle (at least, if he or she is a reasonably sane person who understands the basic laws of physics: moving car + walking person = splat). This fear breeds caution, which causes the person to look both ways for oncoming traffic and wait for an appropriate time to venture across the road.

However, unjustified fear- which can be just as crippling and realistic as justified fear- is more often the case when fear is a factor. Not many people risk their lives on a regular basis. Humiliation, rejection, and failure top the list* of limiting fears that can be overcome with practice and determination.

* Actually, spiders top the list of fears for most people. Arachnophobia- fear of spiders- is the most common type of fear in the world. However, fear of spiders is completely justifiable, as spiders are creepy eight-legged insects with fangs, alien eyes, and a tendency to drop on you out of nowhere.

One of the easiest and most successful methods of dealing with fear is exposure therapy, which is actually facing your fears one small step at a time. If you don't feel you can handle exposure therapy alone, enlist a friend to participate- especially if you can find a friend who doesn't fear the same things you do. With exposure therapy, the objective is to experience fear to a small degree several times, so that each time it becomes easier to conquer. (Please note that exposure therapy does not apply to every situation. For example, if you are afraid of flying, it is not recommended that you leap from successively higher perches and attempt to become airborne.)

Here are some ways you can implement exposure therapy for the Big Three fears:

Humiliation

- Wear your slippers to the grocery store. If you're feeling ultra-brave, scuff your feet across the floor to call attention to your slippers. If you're feeling ultra-timid, go to a grocery store far enough from your house that the shoppers will probably never see you again.

- Sing at a karaoke bar. While you"re sober.

- Choose one completely inappropriate article of clothing (a Dr. Seuss hat, a big pair of fuzzy mittens in the middle of summer, a headband with bumblebee antenna) and wear it in public as long as you can. This is not only good exposure therapy- it"s fun!

- Join a local Toastmasters club or offer to give a public presentation on an area relating to your expertise at a library or school. Public speaking is an excellent channel for exorcising humiliation, especially if you do it on a regular basis (that"s speak in public, not humiliate yourself).

Rejection

- Call up a deejay at a local country radio station and request a song by Metallica or Ozzy Osbourne. Be aware that you *will* be rejected; you might be laughed at and rejected, and there is a possibility you may be laughed at and rejected on the air.

- If you"re single, use an online location service like Classmates.com or PeopleFinder.com to find an old school classmate you used to have a crush on. Contact them and ask for a date (or just initiate a conversation). If you"re married, contact an old school classmate and invite them to lunch. At worst they"ll say no; at best, you will have rediscovered a friend.
- Write a poem or a short story and try to submit it to a newspaper or magazine, or enter a writing contest. If you aren"t rejected, become a writer immediately.

Failure

- Try to nail Jell-o to a tree.
- Buy a new video game and attempt to win it in one sitting. If you play video games on a regular basis, buy a video game that"s different from the ones you usually play (for example, if you enjoy fighting video games, try a quest-driven format. Or video chess.).
- Start a new hobby that requires creating an end product, such as knitting, model kit building, or cake decorating. Please note that if you are working on your dietary habits, it

is not advisable to embark on cake-decorating exposure therapy to combat fear of failure. You will feel obliged to consume your failed attempts. Instead, try vegetable sculpture or fruit bowl arrangement.

- Challenge Jeff Gordon to a stock car race. This will also help overcome your fears of rejection and humiliation, as at least one of them is bound to happen.

Conquering your fears is like climbing a mountain – do it one step at a time.

You can determine your own form of exposure therapy by coming up with ways to face your personal fears one small step at a time. If you can't think of anything, ask a friend to help. Most people are more than willing to try something new, especially if they get to watch you do something entertaining.

NOTE: These exercises are not intended as a substitute for professional psychiatric care. If your fears are extraordinarily strong and interfere with normal functions or daily activities, you should seek the advice of a certified psychiatrist. Self-induced exposure therapy can be effective in reducing or alleviating normal fear, but should not be used in cases of mentally crippling or trauma-induced fear.

Trauma: Breaking the Chains

> **"If you're going through hell, keep going."**
> **- Sir Winston Churchill**

Bad things happen to good people. It"s a fact of life. One of the most extraordinary things about human beings is our capacity for resilience in the face of trauma. Miraculous survival and recovery are not occasional happenings in the world. Every day, someone survives a tragedy. Every day, someone takes another step toward a happier life despite a past trauma. Every day, life goes on, and we adjust. And we are stronger for it.

The suggestions in this section, once again, are not substitutes for professional psychiatric care. However, many people have found self-help effective for relieving the stress of trauma and taking control of themselves. Whether you choose to seek professional help or embark on a healing path yourself, know that you can break free and begin to live again when tragedy touches you. You don't have to let trauma keep you from achieving what you want out of life.

You can choose just one, or any combination of these techniques to work on freeing yourself from trauma. If you are uncomfortable with an approach, move on to another selection.

"It Could Be Worse": Dramatization and Awareness

For mild trauma, sometimes laughter really is the best medicine. If you are able to look at the situation objectively, you may be able to "laugh it off," or at least arm yourself with enough knowledge to realize you had it easy.

There are two ways to approach this method. The first is to simply use your imagination. Picture the trauma, and then imagine all the ways in which it could have been worse. For example, if you have a checking account, you may have bounced a check, ended up having to pay a fee to the bank and had to postpone paying one of your bills or go without something you planned to purchase. Now, imagine what might have happened if you bounced multiple checks. You might have had to put off several payments. The snowball effect could have caused you to lose your car, or have your power shut off. Your bills could have spiraled out of control, eventually leaving you homeless.* When you imagine the worst, it"s easier to put setbacks into perspective.

Traumas can be seeds for more pain – or for growth.

*NOTE: Bouncing multiple checks and losing your power, your car, or your house qualifies as major trauma, for which dramatization is not always effective.

The second approach to dramatization and awareness of minor trauma is to research actual cases where the situations of other people turned out worse than yours. You can search online for news stories, or browse the periodicals archive at your local library. Generally, you will always be able to find cases concerning people who had more difficulty than you, yet they survived- and you will too. After all, you"re still alive. If you want to take this method a step further, you can do something to help others in your situation. Make a donation to a specific case or a related charity, or start a support program or fund drive in your community. Taking action, no matter how small, often helps to alleviate the feelings of loss and helplessness associated with trauma.

For Your Eyes Only: Journaling to Release

Keeping a journal or diary is one of humankind"s oldest traditions. The thoughts, feelings and emotions of generations have been preserved through countless pages inscribed with words that are often kept private throughout the life of the writer, and revealed only in the interests of adding to historical record.

For therapeutic purposes, sometimes the act itself of writing down past trauma allows you to face it more fully and release the negative feelings associated with the event. The journaling process can be a short-term program used solely for working on a specific trauma. If you keep a short-term journal, you may wish to burn or destroy it at the end of the process as a symbolic realization of your freedom from trauma. If you enjoy journaling, you may wish to continue keeping a written record of your thoughts and feelings. Many people keep daily or weekly journals their entire lives. Journaling is an excellent form of self-communication that can benefit you whether or not you've experienced trauma in your life.

There are many different formats your journal can take. Following are some of the most common, but feel free to come up with your own journaling style to suit your specific needs:

- **Freeform thought.** Freeform writing is a technique used by many authors and aspiring authors to jumpstart creativity. Keeping a freeform journal is a good way to uncover thoughts you may be hiding even from yourself, and for beginners it's an excellent starting point. The instructions for writing freeform are simple: just sit down with your journal and writing implement of choice, and start writing. Don't worry about spelling, grammar, or even coherence. Simply write down whatever comes to mind. Try to do this for at least five minutes to give your mental engines time to warm up. If you don't feel like stopping after five minutes, just keep writing. Daily freeform writing is one of the most therapeutic practices available.
- **Memory release.** This technique is most beneficial for short-term journaling, particularly if you intend to destroy the

journal in a symbolic manner when you"re finished. Memory release journaling is exactly what it sounds like: you merely write down your memories of trauma and any feelings associated with them, and then release those negative feelings. Imagine that they are now on paper, and therefore no longer in your heart or mind. For this reason, it is more effective to destroy the journal when you are finished with it.

- **Dear Jerk letters.** If a specific person or group of people, living or dead, was responsible for the trauma in your life, writing a letter or series of letters to them can be helpful in transcending your trauma. You will probably never send them the letters, but putting down in physical form what you would say to them if you could is immensely satisfying on a personal level. You can address the letters to their names, or give them creative nicknames (Dear Jerk, Dear Friend-Stealer, Dear Scum of the Earth) to protect your privacy and add more kick to your scathing monologues.

- **Story-form therapy.** Some traumas are too fresh or too painful to relive fully. In these cases, writing a fictionalized account of the experience can be helpful in releasing negative emotions. You can change the names, locations, ages, or even genders of the participants in your personal trauma to give yourself a more objective view of the situation and assist you in coping or finding closure. Creating alternate versions of the situation helps to displace bad feelings. You can even write yourself a happy ending, or give your fictional self victory over your oppressor.

- **Pictorial journals.** You may feel words are inadequate to convey your traumatic emotions. If this is the case, you might consider drawing a journal instead. Just as you don't have to be a good writer to keep a journal, you don't have to be a good artist to draw one. Use whatever form you feel comfortable with, whether it is stick figures, abstract scribbling, or fully detailed rendering. The only important step in journaling is to get something concrete down on paper, and no one but you will ever have to look at it.

Choosing the right journal can be just as important as what you place inside it. The human mind is a powerful thing, and our thoughts and perceptions have an incredible influence on our actions. Here are a few tips on choosing an appropriate journal for your self-guided therapy:

- The size, layout, look and feel of your journal should be symbolic, either of your intentions or your personality. Take your time in picking out a journal you enjoy looking at and holding. Give yourself permission to spend a little more than you usually would, and avoid bargains or sales (unless the one on sale is exactly what you"re looking for). Attaching a slightly higher dollar value to your journal than what you might pay for something like a typical school-grade spiral notebook gives the importance of your journal a mental boost, and helps remind you that what you put inside it is important to you. If you don"t want anyone else to read your journal, no matter what, invest in one with a lock.
- Choose a writing implement that you will use specifically for your journal. With the exception of a pictorial journal, pencil is the poorest medium to use, as it conveys the sense of a temporary state that can be changed with a pass of the eraser. Pen or marker are the best choices. You should write with the medium you feel most comfortable in, that benefits you in a symbolic or significant way. You can choose an ink color you like, buy a set of glitter pens, pick

up a novelty pen, or even get an old-fashioned quill pen- they are available in ballpoint versions or traditional chisel-point and inkwell styles. Be sure to only use the writing implement you choose for your journal, and not for grocery lists or jotting down phone numbers.

- Find a home for your journal and keep it there unless you"re writing in it. Establishing a permanent place for your journal- under the bed, on the top shelf in the closet, in a dresser drawer, on your nightstand- is an important step in your journaling routine. This helps to reinforce permanence and form new habits (and eliminates the possibility of losing your journal).

Meditation: Connecting Above Pain

Meditation is a time-honored relaxation technique that has been used successfully in Eastern cultures for centuries to alleviate stress and focus the mind. This technique has recently gained popularity in the United States as millions of people discover both the physical and mental health benefits of meditation, while realizing that it"s not as difficult as it sounds.

In trauma applications, meditation can help you rebuild the energy your negative emotions zap and learn to cope with the difficulties associated with trauma. Meditation is one of the easiest and most inexpensive forms of self-therapy: all you need is yourself and a quiet room.

There are several variations of meditation you can perform. You should choose the steps or combination of steps you"re most comfortable with and use them on a regular basis. Following are a just a few of the hundreds of meditation forms in existence; or you can combine elements of different meditation programs to create your own unique method.

NOTE: In all methods of meditation, the object is to clear your mind of conscious thought and concentrate on simply existing in the moment.

Walking Meditation: When you perform walking meditation, you can meditate and exercise at the same time. To meditate while walking, you simply concentrate on either the feeling of your foot meeting the earth with each step, or on your breathing, which should be relaxed and natural. Achieving concentration in order to block out thought takes practice, but the natural rhythm of walking provides an excellent starting point for the beginning meditation student.

Standing Meditation: Performing standing meditation is a good way to practice proper breathing, as a standing position is conducive to correct posture and fully open airways. To practice standing meditation, stand straight and comfortably with your feet pointed forward, approximately a shoulder-length apart. Place your hands one over the other on your lower abdomen and concentrate on breathing. Take slow breaths and hold for about four seconds before releasing slowly. Proper meditation breathing is done through the nose, both in and out. Standing meditation can be performed with your eyes open or closed, according to your preference.

Seated Meditation: This is the most popular form of meditation. In a quiet room, be seated either in a comfortable chair with your feet flat on the floor, or on the floor in a cross-legged position (usually Indian or Lotus). As with standing meditation, you can concentrate on breathing and slowly empty your mind of thought. Seated meditation is performed with relaxed, open eyes focused on a fixed point on the floor approximately three feet in front of you. Many practitioners of seated meditation use external stimuli for concentration (see "Meditation with External Stimulus).

Reclined Meditation: Reclined meditation is best performed just before you intend to go to sleep, as often you will find yourself falling asleep as you do it. This variant is the same as standing meditation, only lying down. The eyes are always closed with reclined meditation. This is a helpful technique for people who have trouble falling asleep.

Some forms of meditation are best done at the end of the day, when it won't matter if you fall asleep.

Meditation with External Stimulus: If you cannot (or would rather not) focus on breathing, you might consider using an external stimulus to focus your thoughts for meditation. One traditional example of external stimuli is a mantra: a word or phrase that is repeated either aloud or silently throughout the meditation session. Some of the more popular meditation mantras are Buddhist or Indian in origin, such as *om* or *aum* (OHM: no English translation); *om mani padme hum* (OHM mah-nee pah-d-may HUNG: the jewel of the lotus); or *rama* (RAH-muh: chant used by Gandhi). You can also create your own mantra with a meaning significant to you or your trauma. Other external stimulus used in meditation are: candles or incense; instrumental music or recorded chants; fans or white noise machines; small fountains; or recorded nature sounds such as waterfalls, bird calls or whale songs. You can use whatever you"d like, as long as it is soothing and relaxing to you.

Join the Club: Live and Online Support Groups

You may be surprised to learn that whatever type of trauma has affected your life, there is probably a support group of people who have been through the same thing and are willing to talk about it with you. Many kinds of trauma are difficult to discuss with anyone who hasn't had the same experience. Support groups are created with that truth in mind.

If your trauma is a common one, such as alcohol abuse, there may be a live support group that meets regularly in your area you can attend. Most churches, community organizations and local newspapers provide lists of area support groups with meeting times, locations and contact information for the coordinators of the group. If there are no live support groups in your area, you might consider forming one. You can find guidelines for forming support groups at your local library or online.

Even if the support you"re looking for is not so common, the internet has allowed people all over the world to connect and unite who might otherwise never have known anyone else like them existed. There are communities, forums and private chat groups online to cover just about every walk of life, from displaced homemakers to victims of sexual abuse to reformed ex-convicts. With careful research, you can find a supportive and friendly internet community to share your trauma with and connect on a level that would otherwise prove difficult, or even impossible, for someone who hasn't experienced a similar event.

Drop That Horseshoe: There's No Such Thing as Bad Luck

> *"Depend on the rabbit's foot if you will, but remember it didn't work for the rabbit."*
> *- R. E. Shay*

Have you broken a mirror in the past seven years? Any black cats crossed your path lately? In nearly every culture, in every part of the world, there are some things attributed to luck: the chance happening of good or bad events, also known as fortune or fate. Luck is used as the rationalization for any number of seemingly inexplicable circumstances. A gambler winning game after game at a casino table is said to be "riding a lucky streak" (though his winnings can likely be attributed at least in part to skill); a homeless person is deemed "down on his luck" (though there is almost certainly a concrete, albeit unfortunate, circumstance behind his tragic state); an individual for whom things always seem to go right is ascribed "the luck of the Irish" (and just what, pray tell, is so lucky about Ireland?).

Those who subscribe to the luck theory and observe superstitions such as avoiding the number 13 and tossing salt over the left shoulder when it spills will insist that it works. For them, it does work; however, this is merely a testament to the power of the mind to persuade us to see what we wish to see. Luck works in much the same way as positive thinking. If you believe you are "safe" because you avoid opening umbrellas in the house and walking under ladders, then you will be safe. On the other hand, if you break a mirror and convince yourself that bad luck is destined to infect you, you will subconsciously sabotage yourself and therefore attract bad luck- or at the least, chalk up unfortunate events to the breaking of the mirror instead of discovering what really happened so you can prevent a reoccurrence of the problem. Seven years is a long time to wait for your luck to change.

It's your time – how will you spend it?

Instead of rubbing the bellies of pregnant women or hoping to find heads-up pennies lying around, why not try positive thinking? You will achieve the same results, and you won't have to rely on discovering four-leaf clovers or avoid stepping on sidewalk cracks. Using the power of positive thinking is as simple as believing good things can and will happen to you. You don't have to memorize a complicated set of rules or follow elaborate rituals to attract happiness and success. So toss that lucky tee shirt from high school and tap in to positive thinking today. Your bad luck sentence is officially discharged.

Change Your Mind, Change Your Life

"Most folks are about as happy as they make up their minds to be."
- Abraham Lincoln

When tapping in to the power of positive thinking, the most important step is to create a mindset that allows you to think positively. Once you have pulled the weeds from your mental garden, you can begin to sow the seeds that will anchor your new way of life.

Creating a positive mindset takes training. In much the same manner as runners train their bodies to endure long periods of sustained activity, you can train your mind to sustain positive thought, and naturally defer to pleasant or optimistic paths. At first, thinking positively may feel awkward or ridiculous (particularly if you"re the type of person who believes perky morning people should be shot). Keep in mind, though, that it does get easier the more you do it, and eventually, sustaining a positive mindset will be as natural as breathing.

Like any training program, there are steps you can follow to achieve your optimal results: in this case, a positive mental outlook. You may recall that it takes 21 days to form a new habit (what"s that...you"ve forgotten already? Go back and add "long-term memory" to your list of habits you"d like to improve). Therefore, you should perform each of the steps for at least 21 consecutive days. You can take on one step at a time, or implement the whole program; just be sure you aren"t leaving anything out.

Step up to your mental treadmill, and let the training begin!

Warm-up: Shake Out Negative Kinks

When you think about it, it's obvious: negative is the opposite of positive, so in order to instill a positive mindset you need to get rid of negative thoughts. Sounds simple enough, right? The process is an easy one, but it takes practice to make it stick.

The first step in clearing negativity from your mind is to really pay attention to your thoughts. Whenever the words *can't, shouldn't, wouldn't, won't, not,* or *never* enter your mind, concentrate on what you're thinking and turn it around to eliminate the negative wording. For example:

Your spouse and children are gone for a few hours, and you have the place to yourself. You're indulging in one of your favorite activities. In the midst of your enjoyment, you start to feel guilty. You think: I really shouldn't be doing this. I could be getting started on the project I promised someone else I'd take care of. *Your enjoyment starts to fade, and you stop what you're doing, resentful that you have to tackle this boring project when you have so little time to yourself...*

Does this sound familiar? The moment you hear yourself think *shouldn't*, stop right there and change direction. In this scenario, you might instead think *I really should be doing this. Taking time for me is important, and when I'm relaxed and satisfied I will be able to do a better job on that project I promised someone else. I'm so glad I got the opportunity to do something I enjoy.*

Try to do this every time a negative thought creeps in. The more often you banish negative ideas from your mind, the easier positive thinking will become. You will be more relaxed and receptive to positive solutions.

Work Those Mouth Muscles

If a picture is worth a thousand words, then a smile is worth a million. The power of a smile is incredible. Even if you don't feel like smiling, the simple act of lifting the corners of your mouth can help you lift your entire spirit and find something worth smiling about. Some of the greatest self-help advice out there comes from those who advocate "fake it until you make it." This is especially true when it comes to positive thinking, and faking a smile goes a long way toward producing the genuine thing. You may end up laughing at yourself merely because you know you have nothing to smile about.

Another great thing about smiles- they"re highly contagious. A smile spreads faster than a cold in a daycare. Most people can"t help smiling back when someone casts a happy expression their way. This is a simple and exciting theory that you can test out for yourself. Go to any public place and start smiling at random people, then keep track of how many smile back (even suspicious smirking counts!). You"ll likely find that 9 out of 10 of your targets return your joyful expression to some small degree, and you"ve probably just made their day a little brighter, too.

Learning to smile on demand is an important step in developing a permanently positive mindset. One good technique for summoning smiles is to choose a happy memory that never fails to fill you with good feelings. Keep this memory at the front of your mental catalogue, and access it whenever you feel a case of the blues coming on. It may not solve your problems, but it will at least make you smile- which in turn helps you relax and take an objective look at your situation.

Smiling often creates a mental cue for the foundation of positive thinking and helps prime the pumps of happiness.

You should also spend a little time in front of the mirror observing your own expressions. At first this practice may seem uncomfortable or downright silly, but smiling at your own reflection has a positive effect on your psyche. You can even practice different smile variations: the amused smirk; the close-lipped leg-pulling smile; the toothy grin; the laugh-out-loud open-mouthed smile. Think of it as an Olympic event...it's your personal Smile Marathon, and you'll win the gold every time!

Do Some Reps

When developing a positive mindset, the importance of repetition cannot be understated. Exercise is the key to building any muscle, so by viewing your optimistic outlook as a muscle, you can develop a reserve of happiness that will carry you through the most grueling events.

This is not to say you shouldn't worry about anything. Ignoring troubling events won't make them go away. It's important to face your problems *while looking at them through a positive lens.* The positive mindset itself doesn't erase your troubles. It is simply a tool to allow you to find a solution without burning yourself out through stress and anxiety. You will find it far easier to solve problems when you can step back and look at the situation in a positive light; and often the solution will present itself with little effort, simply because your mind is clear and open enough to notice it.

The more you practice positive thinking, the more naturally it will come to you. You will find that frustrating everyday occurrences dwindle to minor nuisances, and eventually cease to trouble you altogether. Keep practicing positive thought processes, and you will be well on your way to a low-stress, high-energy lifestyle that will allow you to accomplish anything you desire.

An incredible achievement – practiced and visualized a million times.

Cool-Down: Feel the Burn

As you come to the end of your daily positive thinking workout, look back and reflect on your progress. Was there anything that seemed easier to you? Were you able to find a faster solution to a problem that would have ordinarily eaten up a lot of time in worrying? Do you feel more relaxed and ready to try again tomorrow?

Congratulate yourself on your victories. By reinforcing your accomplishments, you help to firm the foundation of your new positive mindset and lay the groundwork for your success. Every positive thought brings you one step closer to your ultimate goal. You will soon realize that you can do this, and you will have much greater enthusiasm as you proceed.

Now that you"ve planted the seeds for positive thinking, the next step is to learn how to care for your mental garden. In the next section you will discover the fuel you need to nurture your seeds and coax new shoots from the soil of your mind. Meanwhile, keep pumping that positive thinking iron!

Switching Terminals: Hook Up to Positive Energy

"No pessimist ever discovered the secret of the stars, or sailed to an uncharted land, or opened a new doorway for the human spirit."
- Helen Keller

Enthusiasm is the sunshine of your mind"s garden. Possessing enthusiasm for all that you do is essential to the process of positive thinking. Just as plants require sunlight to develop and grow, utilizing the power of positive thinking requires enthusiasm to energize your potential and ensure an endless supply of fuel.

You will discover that the more enthusiasm you generate, the more energy you"ll have to put in. There are some things it will be easy to generate enthusiasm over, and others where you"ll have to stretch yourself to find what will spark your enjoyment. For example, no one has trouble generating enthusiasm for spending an unexpected bonus from work or taking a night out. However, you may find it hard to get excited about washing dishes or filling out your income tax forms. But part of the magic of positive thinking is developing the ability to find the good things in any situation and use them to get through the difficult parts.

Like developing a positive mindset, enthusiasm must be cultivated and sheltered from potentially damaging emotional storms. There are several methods you can use to put a dose of passion into everything you do, whether it"s finally taking that dream vacation or scrubbing out the basement. You can choose the method that best fits whatever situation you"re facing and ensure yourself the energy to tackle anything life happens to throw at you.

What's In It for Me?

One of the most elemental solutions for finding enthusiasm is to focus on the benefit you will derive from completing a particular task. In some situations it"s easy to discover the benefit. For instance, you may hate wrapping presents, but you know the person you"re giving the present to will be overjoyed when presented with this lovely paper-wrapped gift, and so you derive happiness from envisioning the recipient opening the present. This is an especially useful tactic when you"re still up at 2 a.m. on Christmas morning trying to figure out how to wrap the bicycle you've just spent three hours putting together.

Other circumstances will not have such obvious benefits. If you were to find yourself trying to change a flat tire on the side of the road in the middle of a snowstorm (or a rainstorm, if you are fortunate enough to live in a snow-free climate) it would undoubtedly be difficult to find your silver lining. Under stressful circumstances, give yourself permission to think of the wildest benefit you can come up with. Perhaps you were on your way to a party you would rather not have gone to. In that case, your flat tire would give you the perfect excuse to turn around and go back home.

There is some good in every situation, whether it"s in the form of a benefit or a lesson to be learned (Lesson One: Never drive with questionable tires through a snowstorm to a party you didn"t want to attend in the first place). You can harness the power of positive thinking by finding that good and exploiting it, no matter how small or insignificant it may seem.

The Buddy System

If you"re having trouble summoning enthusiasm for a particular task, try to seek out someone who enjoys doing that sort of thing and ask them to partner up with you. Like smiling, enthusiasm is contagious. If you spend some time observing another person"s enthusiasm, some of it is bound to rub off on you.

If you don"t know anyone who might be enthusiastic about what you're trying to accomplish, try going online to look up articles or blogs (web logs, which are usually personal, regularly updated online journals) pertaining to the subject. Sometimes merely reading about someone else"s enthusiasm can help you find some aspect of the task to enjoy, and get you through it with a minimal amount of stress, anxiety and dread. (Be warned: it may be difficult to discover anyone who enjoys scrubbing toilets or emptying cat litter boxes. In these cases, you might be on your own!)

Knowledge is Power

Muddling through a particular task or project can be daunting if you don"t know what you"re doing. If you"re the type of person who never asks for directions or reads the instructions, you may be tempted to take on challenges in areas where your knowledge is limited. Even if you're not, you may find yourself faced with taking on a task you don't feel qualified to handle, whether it's filling in for someone in a different department at work or changing an infant's diaper for the first time.

The more you know about what you're doing, the easier it will be to accomplish. This may seem self-explanatory, but many people don't realize that you can always find out more information. It only takes a few minutes to look up something on the internet, consult a reference book, or call up someone you know has experience with the issue you're facing.

Gaining knowledge has other benefits as well. The more you know about a given subject, the better you will be able to focus on your goal and work toward it. You cannot reach your destination if you cannot find the path. Look upon knowledge as the pruning shears of your mental garden, clearing the way for enthusiasm to grow and spread. With the right set of tools, you can accomplish any task easily.

Sign on the Dotted Line

Being committed to achieving your aim is essential to generating a sense of enthusiasm. Whether you want to have gleaming white teeth or flash your pearly whites at crowds of thousands as you accept your Academy Award, you should be completely committed to what you"re trying to accomplish.

One way to cement your personal commitment is to outline a step-by-step plan for reaching your goals. You can do this with any task, no matter how great or small (though you might save time to generate a mental plan for things like washing the dinner dishes, as it might take you more time to write it all down than it would to actually wash them). On a sheet of paper- or for monumental tasks such as changing careers, at the beginning of a notebook- note your starting point: where you are now. Leave yourself some space, and then jot down where you want to be and how long you plan on taking to get there. Then go back and break down the process of getting from point A to point B in detailed steps. This not only helps you to visualize reaching your goal, it also allows you to cross steps off as you complete them. Your enthusiasm will be sustained as you move further toward your goal.

While you"re writing things down, consider creating a contract with yourself to reach your objective. You can even ask a friend or family member to act as a witness, which will further solidify your intentions to follow through. Your contract can be a simple document stating your promise to yourself, or a detailed map of the things you will do to help yourself reach your aims, with deadline dates for additional motivation and bursts of enthusiasm. Keep your contract posted visibly to remind yourself of your intentions. Every time you see it, you will find yourself eager to achieve your goal and fulfill your contract.

Dangle Your Own Carrot

Ask any business owner and you'll find out that rewards are one of the most powerful motivators. People are more willing to work toward a goal when they know they will get something out of it at the end. Since your boss probably won't reward you for losing weight or remodeling your bathroom, you can plan to give yourself a reward when you meet a given goal.

When selecting self-rewards, be sure to match them to your goals. This will not only ensure you don't get tired of the same reward, but will also help you when you're planning the strategies you'll use to accomplish your aims. For example, if you'd like to spend less time watching television and more time outside or with your family, you can reward yourself with a trip to the theater to see a great movie. If you're planning to quit smoking, part of your strategy could be to set aside some of the money you'll save by not buying cigarettes and get yourself a new outfit, or something you've had your eye on for a while but haven't been able to afford.

Some goals come with intrinsic rewards already built in, yours for the claiming when you reach your objective. For example, if you're going to start your own business, you already know you'll be rewarded by working for yourself, possibly even by working out of your home. Whether you're working for an intrinsic reward or providing yourself with an incentive, treating yourself is a great way to generate enthusiasm for the task at hand.

Surrender

That"s right. Sometimes, you should just give up.

This may not be the type of advice you"d expect to find in a book about positive thinking. However, there is a specific time when you should surrender- and that is when you hate doing what you"re doing.

> **"Like what you do. If you don't like it, do something else."**
> **- Paul Harvey**

Too many people end up settling for the life they think they ought to have, the life others have told them to expect, or the life they believe they"re stuck with. You must realize that there is room on this planet for everyone, and if you"re feeling trapped in a job you despise or a living space you can"t stand, you need to make a change- not down the road, when you have time, or as soon as you get whatever it is you"ve been waiting for; but *right now.* That elusive "someday" is always going to be in the future, and you can"t catch up to the future. *Now* is the only time you have.

This doesn't mean you should drop everything and throw caution to the wind- at least, not in most cases. If you"re like most people, you have responsibilities that must be taken care of. However, there is always something you can do *right now* to cast out your net and catch "someday," and start pulling it toward you. Do you hate your job, but lack the experience to get a different one? Start taking night classes or sign up for an online course. There are hundreds of accredited universities offering distance learning classes over the internet. Is your house or apartment located in a neighborhood that started out great, but is becoming worse every day- and you haven't found the time or the money to move? Take a close look at your budget and see if there"s anything you can do without for a few months, or ask your landlord or bank if they have any other properties you could look into.

Waiting fuels the fires of apathy. Doing something about your situation, no matter how small or insignificant it may seem, can start a chain reaction of enthusiasm that will energize you to reach your goals. You deserve to get what you want out of life while you"re still here to enjoy it. Don't put it off another day, because your "someday" is right now!

SHOOTS AND LEAVES

"Motivation is what gets you started. Habit is what keeps you going."
- Jim Ryan

Now that you"ve planted your mental garden, you will start to see the beginnings of growth in yourself and your surroundings. At this stage, it is important to nurture the tender new beginnings of your confident, positive self. You should learn to recognize the effects of positive thinking in your life and encourage the development of strong roots to anchor yourself in success.

Tenacity helps.

The First Signs of Your Spring of Rebirth

"There's only one corner of the universe you can be certain of improving, and that's your own self."
- Aldous Huxley

As you practice using positive thinking, you will find that things begin to change for you. Sometimes the change is so gradual you don't notice anything at all, until one day someone else tells you that you seem different. They may ask if you've gotten a new outfit, changed your hair, lost weight, or won the lottery. Tapping in to positive thinking not only makes you happier, it also makes you more attractive; the kind of person others want to be around.

Now that you've had some experience, you might recognize some of the common signs of positively charged people. Check out this list of things you have to look forward to.

You Know You're a Positive Thinker When:

- Your grueling drive to work goes by so quickly, you wonder why it ever bothered you in the first place.

- The clerk at the grocery store gives you the wrong change, you point it out with a smile- and she happily corrects the mistake.
- You waited in line at the bank for twenty-five minutes on your lunch hour...and your life didn't end.
- The new part for your car finally arrived at the garage after a week on backorder, but it was the wrong one. You were so nice about accepting the delay when the garage called that they offered you a substantial discount on your repair bill.
- Every time you catch a glimpse of yourself in a mirror, you're smiling- and you don't think you look like a moron.
- You put the oven on too high and burned dinner...then wound up having something even better than you'd planned.
- Suddenly you have a lot more free time on your hands, and plenty of things to do with it- plus enough energy to do them.
- The last time you thought the word *can't* was in the phrase *I can't believe all these great things are happening to me.*

Positive thinking has the power to change your life, as long as you believe it does. As you continue to use positive thinking techniques, you will find you don't have to put much effort into achieving what you want.

Conspiracy Theory: The Biggest Threat to the New You

> *"When a man points a finger at someone else, he should remember that four of his fingers are pointing at himself."*
> *- Louis Nizer*

Every path has its obstacles. Along the road to positive thinking, you will find only one: yourself. Human beings have a tendency to create conspiracies against themselves and impose the self-limiting beliefs that surround them on every aspect of their lives, whether these restrictive ideals result from environment, upbringing, or a combination of influential factors.

You may not even recognize your own self-defeating actions. However, the power to access the benefits of positive thinking rests solely within yourself- and you are the only one that can stand in your way. Therefore, you must learn how to step aside and allow yourself to develop to your full potential.

Following are some of the most common patterns of self-limiting behavior, along with steps you can take to get out of your own way and blaze your personal path to happiness and success.

There's Always Tomorrow: Eradicate Procrastination

> **"To be always intending to make a new and better life but never find time to set about it is as... to put off eating and drinking and sleeping from one day to the next until you're dead."**
> **- Og Mandino**

Procrastination is the easiest thing in the world to perfect- and one of the hardest habits to break. There will always be a good reason to put off whatever you want to accomplish, whether it"s vacuuming the living room carpet or finally taking that European vacation you"ve been planning for years.

When you realize you"re putting something off, one of the best things you can do is to ask yourself why you don"t want to do it. The reasons for procrastination are as varied as the people who practice it: the task is boring or repetitive; you are afraid you won"t be able to handle it; the project is difficult or time-consuming; it is going to be an unpleasant experience; you dread the possible consequences of seeing the task through to completion. Once you know what is stopping you from moving ahead, you can determine your strategy for accomplishing your goal and get un-stuck.

How do you crush procrastination in its tracks? The remedies for moving past procrastination include:

- **Just do it.** Whatever the task you"re facing, simply pick a point and get started. Often things are not as bad as they seem, and once you start doing something it"s easier to build up momentum that will carry you through to the end. Tell yourself that when you finish the unpleasant task, you won"t have it hanging over your head and you can move on to better things.
- **Break it up, people.** Take a few minutes to break up larger tasks into small, manageable goals. For example, if you are attempting to organize your desk at work, you might pick one drawer and get that done, and then take a break and do something else before returning for the next drawer.

Meeting a series of small goals is more motivating and encouraging than trying to tackle a huge project all at once.

- **Cut through the fluff.** Prepare yourself to work through distractions when you"re taking on a task. If possible, ignore the phone- and definitely resist the temptation to play Solitaire or check your e-mail a dozen times. Make sure your mind is made up to do whatever it is you"re doing and nothing else until it"s finished. You will feel better knowing it"s done, and you'll waste less time on sideline projects.

- **Stick to the program.** Ensure you have enough time to finish the task you're starting. If you know you're going to be interrupted or run out of time before you"re through, choose one part of the task to complete instead of trying to rush through the whole thing. Rushing to meet a deadline you know you can't make causes more stress, and can actually make things happen slower because you"re worried that you won't be able to accomplish what you've set out to do. Give yourself a break, and your stress level will thank you.

- **Expect the unexpected.** Despite our best positive thinking efforts, things do occasionally take a turn for the unexpected. Delays are a given in many situations. When you're planning a task or goal, it is important to factor in time in case things go wrong. Delays are a major facilitator of procrastination: it's easy to convince yourself to put things off when you already have to wait. Make sure you have a backup plan in place so you can avoid putting things off and still meet your completion goals comfortably.

Just Say No: How Not to Take On Too Much

"The best executive is the one who has sense enough to pick good men to do what he wants done, and self-restraint enough to keep from meddling with them while they do it."
- Theodore Roosevelt

People are always going to ask you to do things for them. That's life. Often we are asked to make commitments we don't feel comfortable with, don't have time for, or just plain don't want to make- but saying "no" makes us feel even worse than agreeing to something we don't like.

Women especially fall victim to the over-commitment syndrome. You should make it a habit to say "no" more often, particularly when you know that agreeing to take on a certain commitment is going to wreak havoc with your life, even though the little voice in your head is telling you accepting would be the "nice" thing to do. When it comes to your sanity, the nicest thing is to make sure you don't over-extend yourself and end up performing a large number of tasks with substandard results.

You can only fit so much through that door!

The first step in learning to say no is deciding which things you should agree to commit to, and which things are all right to pass on. This decision should stem from your personal priorities; the things that are important to you and your life. This is one reason why it"s important to define your goals clearly when you begin using the power of positive thinking. Weigh each request against your goals and decide whether agreeing to them would move you closer or further away from your objectives.

When you come to a point where you must refuse a request, there are several ways to say no without hurting feelings or making yourself appear inconsiderate. Be as honest as possible when saying no, and you will be able to proceed with a guilt-free conscience.

Need an excuse? Here are the top ten ways to say no nicely:

1. **"No."** Sometimes, the best way to refuse is politely, but directly. If someone in your life is constantly asking you to do things they could easily handle themselves, a firm "no" is the only way to get them to stop. Another approach to problematic people with frequent requests is to tell them, "I know you'll do a great job handling it on your own."

2. **"I'm in the middle of several other projects/commitments right now."** Don't be afraid to tell people when you're busy. Most will respect your schedule and find another way to fulfill their requests for help. You shouldn't be expected to drop tasks you've already committed to in order to complete new ones.

3. **"I need to focus on [my career, my family, my personal life] at the moment."** If you're going through a difficult time in another area of your life that requires your attention, don't hesitate to refuse taking on extra requests. You don't necessarily have to explain your specific reasoning for taking a pass; just indicate that you

4. **"I don't feel I'm the best person to handle that task."** When you don't feel qualified to handle something requested of you, say so. Explain that you don't want to do a poor job, because you know this task is important to the person asking you to do it. Chances are, they want the task done well, too.

5. **"I can't do it, but I know someone else who can."** Only use this "no" form if you truly know someone who can not only handle the task, but has the time to do it. It's nice to be able to offer alternative help, but only if you can follow through on your offer. Referring people to someone else who won't be able to help either will be viewed as a brush-off; the person who originally came to you will think you never actually wanted to help them in the first place.

6. **"I'm not comfortable/don't enjoy doing that."** Stick to your guns. If you're asked to do something that seems wrong or a task you despise doing, don't agree to it and explain why. This way you will be able to avoid repeat requests for the same thing.

7. **"I can't help right now, but ask me later."** Again, be honest with this statement. If you really do want to help out, but just don't have the time when the request is made, let the person asking you know that you'd be happy to help out when you can. If possible, give them a specific availability, like tomorrow or next week, when you know you'll be free. If they need the task done before then, they will find someone else.

8. **"I have no experience with this type of task."** This is similar to stating you're not the best person for the job, but more significant- at least for you. When you take on a task for someone else, you shouldn't have to learn a whole new skill set just to complete one thing. However, if it's something you were planning to learn anyway, you might want to take advantage of the opportunity to learn something new.

9. **"I know you want to [other person's objective] but I can't get away from [other commitment] right now."** This is a polite way to acknowledge the needs of the other person while refusing to overburden yourself. This can also open the opportunity to handle the root issue of the request in a way that is convenient for both of you.

10. **"No, but..."** If for whatever reason you can't commit to a request, you can offer an alternative that would be beneficial to the situation. Perhaps you"re unable to perform the specific task requested, but there is another aspect of the project you would be able to help out with. Again, this leaves your options open without making you seem callous or unconcerned with whomever is making a request of you.

Practice saying no both at home and at work, whenever you"re asked to take on more than you know you can handle. Overextending yourself can be a hard habit to break, but it is an essential step in
getting out of your own way so you can accomplish your life"s goals. You deserve time for yourself, and you must be responsible for ensuring your personal needs are met.

Take Me As I Am: Kicking the Approval Habit

"You cannot be lonely if you like the person you're alone with."
- Dr. Wayne Dyer

Everyone wants approval and acceptance from those we care about. However, too often we depend on approval so much that we lose sight of the most important approval of all: our own.

Do you find yourself agreeing just to avoid disagreeing? Are you constantly seeking out the approval of others before you make a decision? This approval addiction is damaging to your quest for improving your life through positive thinking. By feeding your approval habit, you become less reliant on your own thoughts and feelings, and therefore less in tune with your goals and what is truly best for you. Though it"s nice to have the support of other people, the only person you can make happy one hundred percent of the time is you.

How can you kick the approval habit and stop worrying about what other people think of your actions? Here are several action plans you can follow in order to make sure your people-pleasing prowess is used only where you want it to be, and not as a crutch for social acceptance.

Know Your Code

In order to avoid seeking approval for approval's sake, you have to know your own beliefs and standards. Being aware of what you believe in will help you voice your opinions and choose the right path for yourself, even when others don't agree. Developing a healthy moral code is an important part of the process of positive thinking.

Writing down your moral code can help to cement your ideals and beliefs and serve as a guide for your decision-making process. Think about the issues that are important to you. Do you believe family values come before everything else? Is your career important to you? Where do you stand on politics: would you rather be vocal in your beliefs, or try to make a difference in the background through voting? Your moral code should govern your actions in every situation, and you should never violate your beliefs simply to gain approval from someone else.

Standing up for what you believe in can be an integral part of taking control of yourself and your life. When you stop seeking approval or validation for all of your thoughts and ideas, you become a stronger person- and the people who truly care about you will respect and admire you for it, rather than turning away. Be informed and develop your moral code, then stick to it. You will be surprised at how much better you feel about yourself...and you won't need anyone else to second your opinion.

Graduate from High School

For many of us, the need for acceptance began in high school. The desire to fit in is strong for most teens, and generally when you"re in school there is nothing more important than friends. Once we leave the structures confines of school and enter the adult world, it can be difficult to shake the feeling that you are only a worthy person if you have a lot of friends, or the "right" friends.

As adults, we need to discard the petty social pecking order of our school days. Life is not a popularity contest. It may not surprise you to learn that the most successful adults were social outcasts in school. A large part of the reason for this is because they did not cultivate the acceptance of their peers, they were free to invest in themselves, gaining knowledge and developing strong personalities that did not depend on validation from the "in" crowd.

In case you need proof, check out the following list of successful people who struggled through high school at the bottom of the food chain:

- **Henry Kissinger** was called "a little fatso" by many of his peers.
- Voluptuous actress and model **Heather Graham** was teased constantly for being quiet and physically underdeveloped.
- **Walt Disney** was considered a shiftless dreamer who would never amount to anything by his teachers and fellow students.
- **Eytan Sugarman**- owner of the NYC nightclub *Suede* which is frequented by the likes of Britney Spears, Cameron Diaz, and Leonardo DiCaprio- was a chubby and friendless child whose guidance counselors told him his life would go nowhere.

As an adult, you are much more capable of realizing that peer acceptance doesn't matter outside of high school. You should strive to be true to yourself. Remember, there is a place for everyone- it's a big planet.

Weed Your Friendship Garden

Many of us tend to judge our worth by the number of friends we have. However, this is not always an accurate assessment, and it can be tiring to keep up with your lunch dates and Christmas card lists- particularly when you have friends who you can't be yourself with.

Take some time to evaluate your friendships. Are there people you spend time with who seem to drain you whenever you're around them? Do you constantly feel like a phony when you're interacting with them, and watch the clock until sufficient time has passed so you can excuse yourself from the conversation? Friends are wonderful to have, but some friendships just aren't worth cultivating.

The next time you find yourself trapped in an awkward situation and are afraid to voice your true thoughts, try speaking your mind anyway. It's likely that one of two things will happen: either the person you're talking with will be interested in your opinion and you'll find the conversation moving into genuine territory, or you will notice a sudden drop in temperature and hear those excuses you usually make to escape come from the other person. If the case is the former, you have improved your relationship and can relax around the person; if it"s the latter, you have just rid yourself of an unnecessary drain on your energy and positive thought process.

There is nothing wrong with ending friendships that just aren"t working out. Chances are, the other person will be just as relieved as you are, and you will both be able to strengthen the relationships you have with true friends. It will take some time to cull the weeds from your friendship garden, but it will be worth it for everyone involved. Freeing yourself from damaging relationships helps you kick the approval habit when you no longer have to "fake it" to get along with anyone.

Blood is Thicker than Embarrassment

It"s one thing to sever relationships with friends, and quite another to do the same with family. Most of us are raised with the idea that family is important, and we tend to be more forgiving of family members as well as seek their approval for our actions more often. We are afraid to be ourselves around family members; often because people change, and we fear our close relatives won't like the changes that come into our lives. So we are forced to continue acting as if we are the same people we were five, ten, or fifteen years ago. This produces an uncomfortable relationship at best, and can lead to estrangement or avoidance if left unchecked.

Try to keep in mind that just as you are forgiving of your family members" collective flaws and personality quirks, they will be forgiving of yours. When you truly care about someone, you accept them for who they are and don't judge them on the basis of their thoughts, opinions and habits. Why wouldn't your family extend the same courtesy to you?

Being yourself and not requiring approval from your family may be even more important than doing so with friends. We tend to derive the basis of our self-security level from our interactions with our family, and if we cannot be comfortable around family, that sense of false security spreads into all areas of our lives. If you"ve been hiding some aspect of your personality or belief system from your family out of fear they won't accept you, try easing into your own opinions gradually. You may be surprised to discover that the people who care about you are more accepting than you think. Sometimes, they may have been practicing the same guarded emotional stance as you, and will be just as relieved when it"s finally out in the open.

In any case, you don"t need approval from even your family for the things you want to accomplish. Though it is more difficult to exclude a family member from your life, if it is more damaging to include them, perhaps you should consider putting some distance between yourself and the destructive family member. Many people are content with agreeing to disagree, and in time both of you may come to an understanding. Meanwhile, don"t let your need for approval overshadow your need to be you. Please yourself first, because no one else is going to do it for you.

The Blame Game: Whose Fault Is It, Anyway?

> ***"The reason people blame things on the previous generation is that there's only one other choice."***
> ***- Doug Larson***

We are a society driven by blame. We blame the government for running our lives, and our parents for ruining it. We blame the fast food industry for making us fat, the tobacco industry for giving us cancer, and the justice system for allowing criminals to roam among us while innocent people sit in jail. We blame our children for giving us gray hair, and our schools for equipping our children with the behaviors that make us old before our time. There is no wrong action, great or small, for which we cannot find someone else to blame. The last person we lay blame on is ourselves.

Too often, though, we are the first person we should point to when problems arise.

The government does make the rules- but we are in charge of electing the rule-makers, and most of us don't vote, while the majority of those who do are insufficiently informed. Our parents have an enormous impact on our lives- but they can only raise us as well as they were equipped to by their own parents, and once we become adults we are responsible for our own behavior. We choose to eat too much fast food, smoke cigarettes, and try to get out of punishment when we break the law. Our children reflect our own behavior back at us like living mirrors; and no matter how much of their time they spend in school, their behavior is determined almost exclusively by what we teach them at home.

It is up to each one of us to take responsibility for our lives. Even if the wrongs in our lives were someone else"s fault, we are the one that control our reaction to the situation. When unfortunate events occur in your life, you can choose to be angry and point fingers- or you can choose to do something about it. Be clear on who is to blame for the problems in your life, and take steps to correct the situation.

Making Your Omelet: How to Learn From Your Mistakes

"Remember: you only have to succeed the last time."
- Brian Tracy

Everyone makes mistakes. The good news is: failure can actually be good for you! The best way- and sometimes the only way- to learn how to make changes in your life and reach your goals is by figuring out how *not* to do things.

There is a process you can use to learn from your mistakes. The more you learn, the closer you will be to reaching your goals in life.

Give Yourself Permission

You know you"re going to make mistakes, especially if you"re trying to do something you"ve never done before. In order to be prepared for the inevitability of mishaps and misadventures, tell yourself that when you make a mistake, it"s still okay- and you"re not going to let mistakes stop you.

This is part of the process of instilling a positive mindset. When you know what to expect, it"s harder for surprises to set you back in your journey to reach your goals. Keep in mind that it is all right to make mistakes, and doing so is not the end of the world. The only people who don"t make mistakes are people who don"t try to do anything in the first place. Don"t be the person who regrets never even trying to accomplish your goals because you were afraid of mistakes.

Make Interesting Mistakes

Once again: you"re going to make mistakes. When this happens, you will learn more by making interesting mistakes rather than stupid ones.

You may be wondering what, exactly, is an interesting mistake? The more complex and challenging your ultimate goal is, the more spectacular your failures will be. The person who experiences a spectacular failure is far more likely to realize spectacular success. Here"s a quick example:

STUPID MISTAKE: *Stubbing your toe on the rake you left lying in the yard.*

INTERESTING MISTAKE: *Turning $30 worth of powdered sugar and chocolate chips into inedible bricks while trying to start your candy- making company because you misread the candy thermometer.*

The first mistake will teach you to put your tools away when you"re done using them, but this is something you probably should have already known. The second mistake, however, is far more valuable to you. It teaches you how *not* to read a candy thermometer, and you will never make the same mistake again. Now you"re one step closer to realizing your dream to start a candy making company. What will your next mistake be?

„Fess Up

The ability to admit that you"ve made a mistake is crucial to the learning process. This doesn"t necessarily mean you have to announce your mistake to the world. However, you do have to be honest with yourself. Owning up to your mistakes is important, not only in your attempts to learn from them, but in the entire process of using positive thinking.

When you admit your mistakes to yourself, be careful not to judge your actions harshly. Your thoughts should not be along the lines of *I screwed this up, and I'm never going to get this right.* Don"t let your mistakes teach you not to try. Instead, think *I made a mistake, and now I know not to do that again.* The biggest lesson in making mistakes can be found in your taking responsibility for them, and then doing something to correct what went wrong.

Pinpoint Your Error

"For want of a nail, the horseshoe was lost..."
- Nursery rhyme (anonymous)

Speaking of what went wrong...do you know *why* you made the mistake? You cannot learn anything from your mistakes if you don't know why it occurred. If things go wrong, and it isn't clear to you what happened, backtrack along the path that brought you to the error and figure out where you strayed.

James R. Chiles, in his book *Inviting Disaster: Tales from the Edge of Technology*, relates the sordid tale of a floating dormitory in the North Sea built for offshore oil workers. During one night, the dormitory rolled over in the water and killed over a hundred people. The engineers responsible for building the dormitory raced to find an explanation, and ultimately discovered that one small crack in the support structure, which had been painted over instead of properly repaired, was responsible for the chain of events leading to the disaster.

Discovering the origin of your own mistakes will help you avoid potential disaster. Take the responsibility to investigate your mistakes thoroughly, so you can avoid the snowball effect one small error can have.

Talk About It

Though you don't have to confess your mistakes, it is sometimes helpful to talk over your troubles with a sympathetic ear- particularly if that ear belongs to a person who knows something about the goal you"re trying to reach.

If you"re having trouble getting through something, there is nothing wrong with asking for help. Seek out an expert or someone you know who"s been through the same experience you"re having, tell them what you feel you"re doing wrong, and listen to what they have to say. Often the most valuable advice we receive comes from unexpected sources, so don't hesitate to ask someone else.

Can't find an expert? The simple act of talking to a friend or loved one about your troubles can be the catalyst you need to keep going despite your mistakes. You may be able to work out exactly what you need to change in your approach as you discuss what you"ve been doing aloud; or you might simply end up feeling relaxed, refreshed and ready to tackle the problem again.

Keep Good Records

Mistakes may not seem very amusing to you while you"re making them, but some day you'll be able to look back and laugh. You will also be able to look back and learn. By keeping a detailed log of your progress, mistakes and all, you will have a solid blueprint you can follow over and over again to reach your objectives.
Following is a sample error log. You can use this format, or create your own, as long as you remember how to read it!

ERROR LOG: Replacing interior wall with built-in bookshelves

DAY	PROJECT STEP	LESSONS LEARNED FROM ERRORS MADE
1	Remove existing plasterboard wall	Check to make sure no breakable objects on opposite side before using sledge.
2	Cut, fit and install backing for shelving unit	Be sure entrance door to house is wide enough to accommodate lumber before attempting to bring inside.

3	Install shelf brackets	Measure shelf distance before installing brackets. Nothing fits on 3" wide shelf.
3	Cut and fasten shelves	Do not use rotary saw on couch.
4	Buy new couch	See previous error.

When you follow the process to learn from your mistakes, you will notice exponential growth in your mental garden. Mistakes are part of life; without them, we would have no discovery- and not much to laugh about.

If Your Buds Shrivel, Add More Fertilizer

"Fall down seven times, stand up eight."
- Japanese proverb

Like any program, there may come a point in your quest to harness the power of positive thinking when you begin to backslide. If your situation becomes extraordinarily difficult, you may be tempted to stop using positive thinking altogether. However, this is absolutely the worst thing you can do.

"Most people achieve their greatest successes one step beyond what looked like their greatest failure."
- Brian Tracy

Hang in there! Remember that the more changes you are trying to make in your life, the harder you will have to work at positive thinking to make them. It will get easier. The best thing you can do if you feel you"re starting to lose ground is to keep thinking positively. This section will discuss things to keep in mind to help you through the rough patches.

When the Door Closes, Go Out the Window

The goals you"ve set for yourself are worth achieving. If you continually run up against obstacles that seem insurmountable, you may be approaching your objectives in the wrong way. There is always a solution to every problem; it just may not be what you expected.

Step back from your situation and try to look at the big picture. Are you throwing yourself repeatedly into a brick wall? If so, maybe instead of trying to burst through the opposition, you could try going around or climbing over it.

One example might be attempting to change jobs. Have you been putting your resume in at every available company, only to be turned down or told there were no positions open? In this case, you might think about your career as a whole.

Your current job may be a little too high-stress for your long-term satisfaction.

Are you truly satisfied doing what you"re doing? If you are, perhaps there are similar jobs in other industries you could look into. If not, you may want to consider abandoning your search for the same job at a different company and start training yourself for a whole new career. It"s never too late to start doing what you love, and those brick walls may be telling you that the path you're trying to follow is not the right one for you.

Buried Alive: What to Do When Your Mountain Crumbles

Tragedy can strike any one of us at any time. Life is precarious and unpredictable, and there are any number of events that can trigger a major life change. Company layoffs, a sudden and unexpected move, a crippling accident, or the loss of a loved one can devastate the most carefully laid plans.

If a major trauma occurs in your life while you are trying to pull everything together, the first thing you should do is take some time for yourself. If you attempt to keep going as though everything is fine and nothing has changed, you will end up burying emotions that will come back to haunt you. Buried pain can poison your mental garden as effectively as arsenic-laced groundwater. It is essential to properly mourn major losses in life, if only so you can fully realize what is missing and learn to compensate for it.

When enough time has passed to allow you to view the situation with more objectivity, review the traumatic event using the lens of positive thinking. What was the bright side of the situation? Were there any lessons to be learned from it? How did the event change you, and can you use that change to become a stronger, more confident person?

Facing tragedy when it occurs is an essential step in your ability to persevere during rough times. You don't have to hide from tragedy- but you also don't have to let it crush your spirit and sap your energy. Mourn your losses when they occur, but develop the ability to discern when it"s time to move on.

Using Your Lifelines

Do you have a support network? When your good intentions start to slide off your path to success, it is helpful to have friends and family you can turn to and share your troubles with. Hearing words of encouragement, especially from people who know what you"re trying to accomplish, can provide you with the impetus you need to keep going, even when a bend in your tunnel prevents you from seeing the light at the end.

You should also be able to call on yourself and your own reserves of energy to carry you through difficult times. If you made a contract with yourself to reach a certain goal, go back and review it. Have you stuck to your original intentions, or have you drifted away from your success blueprint? One advantage to having a detailed plan to reach your goals is the ability to go back and figure out where you were led astray, and retrace your steps so you can return to your intentions. If you"ve discovered along the way that your goals have changed, you can map out a new path and start at the beginning.

Have you been keeping your journal? If you start to lose faith in the power of positive thinking, try looking back and reflecting on all that you have accomplished so far. Even if things are hard for you right now, you should have already proven to yourself that positive thinking works fairly well for being a bunch of crap. Don"t be afraid to pile on a new load of fertilizer when your first crop doesn"t make it all the way.

Whether you"ve had a few false starts or discovered your natural green thumb, you should soon be well on your way to the harvest, which is the realization of everything you want out of life. Your tender shoots will develop into sturdy plants; able to weather the worst storms life manages to send your way. You are about to see the first blossoms of your efforts, bursting from the melting crust of your former self like daisies in the spring.

OPENING YOUR BLOSSOMS

"Opportunity rarely knocks on your door. Knock rather on opportunity's door if you ardently wish to enter."
- Charles Forbes

Now that your new positive mindset is firmly rooted in your mental garden, you will start to see the buds of possibility appearing everywhere in your life. You can learn to coax blossoming success from the endless fertile fields surrounding you. Recognizing opportunity is an essential component to achieving your objectives; whether is it subtle as a clover or brilliant as a sunflower.

In this section, we will review tips and techniques for realizing the full potential of the power of positive thinking

Poppy Fields: Visualizing in Technicolor

"We must be over the rainbow!"
- Dorothy Gale in The Wizard of Oz

Anyone who has seen the timeless classic film *The Wizard of Oz* remembers that magical moment when Judy Garland"s Dorothy steps out from the wreckage of her black-and-white house into a breathtakingly colorful world- a world she later discovers had been there all along. Realizing the power of positive thinking is like capturing that movie magic for yourself. Suddenly, your surroundings appear in a whole new light: alive with the possibilities of your life and ripe for picking.

One powerful method for accessing positive thinking is visualization. This means picturing yourself actually achieving your goals and being the person you want to be. Like many of the processes we have described so far, using visualization can feel awkward at first. The best way to start off using visualization is solo practice, but eventually you will be able to initiate the process of visualization in just about any circumstance, under any conditions.

The most important thing you should learn about visualization is this: it only works if you really, *really* want it to work. Whatever you are visualizing, whether it"s a material goal or a new mental attitude, you must be absolutely convinced of your vision. This method runs on mental energy, so the stronger your thoughts are, the more likely they will be to influence your life.

Shoot the works – visualize something beautiful.

Preparation: Boarding the Visualization Train

There are several varieties of visualization methods, but the first step in any one of them is always the same. You must prepare yourself mentally to receive your vision in order to be able to fully immerse your consciousness. The process of preparing for visualization is nearly the same as meditation, and you can add in your own elements as you gain more experience with the process.

- **Find a quiet, undisturbed place.** At first you will need to be alone while you visualize. Choose a room or a space that you will use on an exclusive basis for visualization during the beginning stages. Be sure your surroundings are quiet and uninterrupted. White noise is acceptable for visualization, but for most methods you should not use music or recorded sound (you will be visualizing your own sounds!).

- **Get comfortable.** The best way to perform visualization is from a seated position. You can use a comfortable chair or the floor or ground, as long as you seat yourself in a way that will allow you to remain comfortable for at least ten to fifteen minutes.

- **Set a timer.** The effects of visualization vary from person to person, but in some cases it can produce a trance-like state. To ensure you don't end up visualizing the day away, get a silent electronic timer (no ticking!) or set an alarm clock to go off in fifteen to twenty minutes (at this point, you still have a few minutes of preparation before you begin the process of visualization).

- **Relax your body.** If you happen to possess the ability to relax at will; great, do that! If you"re like most of us and you do not, you can engage in progressive relaxation to drain the tension from your muscles. Begin at your feet and concentrate on releasing all tension, one body part at a

  time. It may take you a few tries to do this; don"t worry if it doesn"t happen the first time. It can be difficult to achieve complete relaxation, and in many cases there will be some tension or stiffness remaining. You will find that the more often you practice relaxation, the less tension remains.

- **Clear your mind.** There are a few ways to accomplish this; you should choose the one that works best for you. One way is to imagine a single, benign object such as a white ball or a leaf, and focus entirely on the imaginary object until all your other thoughts simmer down. Picture your thoughts as a crowd in a football stadium, with the object in the center. Each thought stills as its attention is drawn to the object, until they are all silent. Another method for clearing your mind is to "send" your thoughts away by wrapping them in a mental "bubble" and allowing them to drift away from your consciousness.

- **Breathe.** Once you have relaxed your body and cleared your mind, you should perform three to five minutes of deep, concentrated breathing. Try to keep yourself focused on nothing but your breathing; this will relax you even further and prepare your mind to experience visualization.

You can also use this introduction to visualization as an alternate form of meditation. Taking a few moments to relax is always beneficial, and can energize you to face the tasks you"ve set for yourself.

Before you actually begin your preparation activities, you should choose the type of visualization you intend to use and make yourself aware of the process involved. Then you will be able to go directly from preparation to visualization.

Guided visualization

Guided visualization is perhaps the most powerful form available. In this method, you act as the captain of your visionary ship, guiding yourself through the images you conceive as though they were actually happening. When using guided visualization, it is especially important to set your timer, as it is easy to become caught up in your visualized reality.

To perform guided visualization, you need to do a bit of preparation beforehand. Choose a setting or scene in which you feel comfortable and affix the setting firmly in your mind: a sandy beach, a deep forest, or even an open-air mall (if you feel better away from nature and would have a tendency to visualize lots of bugs).

Guided visualization is best for working on your own emotions and behaviors. Decide before you begin the way you want to visualize yourself, whether it is being more confident, losing weight, or simply feeling relaxed and at ease. Tell yourself that the place you"re going will give you the power to achieve these feelings, emotions or characteristics. When you begin your visualization after your preparation phase, don"t imagine watching yourself perform the desired actions. Instead, try to feel as though you are actually doing them: as if you have suddenly lost fifty pounds, or gained a hefty dose of confidence. You might even want to make yourself fly! (Just be sure you don"t try to translate your newfound powers of flight into real life experience, unless it"s boarding a plane).

You can also perform guided visualization with the assistance of an audio program or themed music. You might want to try guided meditation tapes the first few times, and then gradually move away from them until you can perform this method on your own. After all, it is your mind that you are trying to reprogram, and you should fill it with your own thoughts, feelings and emotions in order to reach your personal objectives.

Receptive visualization

Another form of visualization is receptive visualization. This differs from guided visualization in that you are watching yourself rather than doing something. Receptive visualization is a good technique for working on your interactions with other people. For example, if you want to ask someone out on a date, you may visualize yourself doing so flawlessly and convincingly, and then visualize your target agreeing.

Performing receptive visualization is almost like watching a movie in your mind, with you as the director. The beauty of receptive visualization is that when things start to go in a different direction from the way you want them, a simple thought can change everything. You are in complete control, and the more completely and often you visualize a situation, the more likely it will be to happen just the way you pictured it.

After you"ve practiced receptive visualization, you can use it just about anywhere, in any situation. For example, imagine you go to the bank to make a withdrawal, but when you reach the teller you discover there is a problem with your account and you have to speak with a bank manager. While you're waiting, you can visualize your conversation with the manager and mentally resolve the matter in your favor. Then, when you actually do speak to the manager, you will be ready to face the situation calmly and with confidence. More often than not, things will proceed quite similarly to your vision.

Receptive visualization is the most useful method of visualization for everyday events. Because it is versatile and adaptable, you can use receptive visualization to resolve nearly any problem. You will be able to move through each day with a sense of confidence that everything will turn out just as you want it to, and because of your projected confidence, other people will respond to you in a pleasant manner.

Practicing your receptive visualization skills can ease the stresses of daily life, which in turn improves your entire situation.

Beautiful visions can lead to beautiful things.

Altered memory visualization

The final visualization technique we will discuss is altered memory visualization. This form is especially useful in resolving past conflicts and calming anger. In altered memory visualization, you can either "be" the image or watch yourself, whichever you are most comfortable with. The main objective of altered memory visualization is to envision an actual memory and alter the outcome in your mind to reach a better, more satisfying resolution.

You can use altered memory visualization for small issues such as being cut off in traffic, or larger areas like past tragedy or trauma. Again, it is important to use a timer for this method, particularly when working with major traumas. It is too easy to become so immersed in your memories that you cannot shake them.

Whether you choose to watch or participate, begin remembering the event you want to change the way it actually occurred. Try to recall all the sights, sounds and smells just as they were. When you reach an unpleasant point in your memory, direct yourself to react differently from the way you did- or direct the other person to do something different. With practice, you will be able to quickly shift your mental images to a more positive chain of events, and the feelings you formerly associated with your memories will lessen in their effect on you. Using altered memory visualization is a powerful tool for forgiveness, whether you direct it toward yourself or someone else.

By employing visualization techniques and practicing frequently, you will heighten and augment your positive thinking foundation. Envisioning your desires is the first step to achieving them. You can accomplish anything you believe you can, and visualization will help you realize your goals faster and with less effort.

Worry-Me-Nots and You-Can-Themums

**"Sooner or later, those who win are those who think they can."
- Richard Bach**

Believing in yourself and your abilities is absolutely the most important thing you can do on your journey to positive thinking. It is critical to develop the self-confidence you need to carry you through to the realization of your goals.

Self-confidence is a bit different from self-esteem. Self-esteem refers to your feelings about yourself, your behaviors and your worth as a person. Self-confidence is your belief in your abilities and in the way you present yourself to the world. The actions of others are more likely to erode your self-confidence rather than your self-esteem. However, the two emotions have quite a bit in common. Both are measures of your inherent or developed belief in yourself- and both can be easily pushed off balance, resulting in either over-confident or defeatist behaviors that distance you from your ultimate objectives.

What will you plant in your garden?

As previously discussed, you need to create a balance between too little self-confidence and too much. You cannot accomplish anything without self-confidence; on the other hand, too much self-confidence can ensure that you don't try hard enough to reach your goals, and you will fall short of realizing your possibilities.

Once you understand that you truly can do anything you put your mind to, you will have unlocked the key to positive thinking. There is no limit to the power of the human mind. Your possibilities really are endless.

You can help yourself build self-confidence through a simple daily exercise you develop yourself after learning the basic premise. Like most of the practices for working with positive thinking, you may feel ridiculous at first (yes, we are aiming to make you feel ridiculous. Next we break out the flowered hats and funny nose glasses). Here are the basic steps to your daily self-confidence routine, which is best performed in the morning as you prepare to face the day:

- **Decimate distractions.** You need this time to yourself. You *deserve* this time to yourself. While you"re performing your self-confidence routine, don"t answer the phone, check your e-mail, watch television, or listen to the radio. Let household members know that this time is your time, and you would prefer not to be disturbed.
- **Get physical.** Pamper yourself with your daily physical preparations. When you shower, use your favorite soap or scented body wash. Choose clothing that makes you feel good and matches your mood. Make yourself comfortable with the way you look, and your self-confidence will rise to match it.
- **Focus forward.** As you get ready, reflect on what you want to accomplish for the day. Be sure to consider the mood you want to set for yourself as well as any goals or objectives

you will reach. You might even partake in a quick receptive visualization session to see yourself reaching your goals and cement them in your mind.

- **Get pumped.** Now comes the ridiculous part. Stand in front of a mirror, look yourself in the eyes, and sing your own praises. Out loud. Tell yourself that you are the person you want to be; that you possess worthwhile qualities; that you can do that which you are now setting out to do. Be as specific as possible. Instead of saying, "I am competent," say: "I know how to handle problems when they arise." The more specific you are, the more effective your self-confidence routine will prove to be.

Self-confidence is the glue that holds your personality together. If you are serious about changing your life, developing a healthy self-confidence will equip you to do it quickly and effortlessly. Don't let fear, worry and doubt keep you from blossoming into confidence. You can accomplish anything, as long as you believe you can. It really is as simple as that.

Cross-Pollination: How to "Bee"

"Our attitudes control our lives. Attitudes are a secret power working twenty-four hours a day, for good or bad. It is of paramount importance that we know how to harness and control this great force."
- Tom Blandi

Perhaps as important as what you believe is the manner in which you believe it. Your attitude can turn a miserable event into a pleasant one; or a good time into a nightmare. By controlling your attitude, you have the power to control any situation and make what you want from it.

In order to determine the best attitude for any given situation, you should take some time to decide the kind of person you want to be, and the image you want to convey. You may be interested in being the life of the party, the quintessential sympathetic ear, or the strong and silent type with the ability to take the lead at any moment. Once you are aware of your true self, you can begin to adjust your attitude to match.

Here are some important considerations to keep in mind as you develop your personal attitude preferences:

Bee yourself

**"He who trims himself to suit everyone will soon whittle himself away."
- Raymond Hull**

Whatever attitude you choose, be sure it is a reflection of your true self. Being true to yourself is crucial to the success of your positive thinking program. You have only one life to live, and spending it trying to emulate someone else robs the world of the person you could have been.

You may not know yourself as well as you would like to, or as well as you should. If you have been following the methods in this book so far, you may have discovered more than you knew before. One of the most wondrous aspects of humankind is that there is always something new to discover about ourselves; always some new avenue of interest to explore or stand to take. We possess the capacity to never succumb to boredom. It is amazing that with all the activity happening in the world, so many people experience lulls and cannot find anything to occupy themselves with. If you ever become bored, you have stopped developing as a person and should take steps to rectify the situation immediately. Knowing yourself is a constant journey that should never cease.

How can you get to know yourself better? Try some of the following techniques to discover aspects of your personality you may not have even known existed:

- **Date Yourself.** Choose an activity you either know you enjoy or believe you will enjoy, and make a date to do it by yourself. Treat this date as you would any other commitment: dress nicely, arrive on time, and don't put it off unless an absolute emergency comes up. When you go out on your date, notice the things that make you feel good. Enjoy the experience of being with yourself and doing something fun. When you are finished, reflect on the date just as you would with any other event. What did you enjoy about the experience? What did you dislike? What would you have changed? You should make a date with yourself at least once a month, even if it"s just for a walk in the woods or an evening on the couch with popcorn and rental movies.

- **Talk to Yourself.** You are capable of making intelligent conversation with other people to discover more about them. Why not do the same with yourself? You can hold a conversation with yourself aloud or in your head, whichever you are comfortable with. Ask yourself leading questions, and then take some time to think about the honest answers. Lying to yourself is the worst offense you can commit.

- **Record Yourself.** When you discover new aspects of your personality or sparks of interest you didn't know you had, write them down and remember them. You may not have time to explore a particular thought when it occurs to you, but if you jot it down and come back to it later, you will be able to expound on it. It can be helpful to keep a small notebook or planner with you to write things down as they occur to you, and flip through it when you have a few spare minutes.

- **Analyze Yourself.** The way you react to social situations and world events can be very revealing about yourself. Keep yourself informed about what"s going on in the world, either by reading the newspaper, watching television news, or frequenting news feed web sites. Take note of your reactions to real events and situations, and try to apply them to situations in your life. You can use this to help you determine why you feel a certain way about people or situations that impact your everyday life, and then plan your attitude toward them around your newfound knowledge.

Bee happy

***"Happiness is not something you postpone for the future; it is something you design for the present."
- Jim Rohn***

Perhaps you are one of those people who are thinking just now, "You can't tell me to be happy. I don't have to be happy if I don't want to be. Isn't this supposed to help me find my true self? What if I'm just not a happy person?" If you are one of those people, think about this: not being happy makes you happy.

Aren't you happy now?

"Happy" is an extremely subjective emotion. What makes one person happy will not necessarily please someone else. You have to define your own happiness, and strive to achieve that state whenever possible.

Happiness is also contagious. A little bit of joy goes a long way, and has a snowball effect- because when you are happy, it makes those around you happy; then they in turn spread the happiness to others. Finding happiness in whatever you do is a large part of generating a permanently positive attitude.

It is a waste of time to do things that will not ultimately make you happy. When you find yourself faced with an unpleasant task that must nevertheless be accomplished, setting your attitude to "happy" will ensure the task is accomplished with minimal stress and maximum results. Alternately, if you have the choice to do something, and you know it won't make you happy, exercise your developing skills in saying "no." Nothing can make you unhappy if you choose not to allow it to. This is the power of positive thinking.

Finding happy. Need some help locating your spring of happiness? Try a few of these methods for tapping happy:

- **Act like a child.** Children are generally the happiest creatures on Earth. Engaging in the activities you loved as a child is a wonderful way to generate a sense of the carefree happiness you enjoyed. Blow bubbles, swing as high as you can, run across the grass just for the sake of running, do somersaults or jumping jacks, or spin in place until you get so dizzy you fall down. A regular dose of childlike joy is a healing balm for your soul. Be uninhibited!

- **Build a treasure box.** Material reminders of happy can be a wonderful jumpstart to your happiness reserves. If you have small tokens of vacations you enjoyed, pleasant notes from friends or loved ones, or significant items you picked up here and there "just because," consider creating a box to keep them in so you can go through it whenever you feel an attack of the blues coming on. A great addition to your treasure box would be something that captures your favorite smells. Scent is the most powerful emotional trigger there is, and the ability to experience a smell with positive connotations can lift your spirits far more effectively than anything else.

- **Love the little things.** The importance of little things that make you happy cannot be underestimated. A favorite book, the sound of your child"s laughter, the scent of fresh popcorn or wet earth after the rain; any of the hundred small things you take pleasure in can be accessed to generate happiness. Keep a mental list of your favorite little things and draw on them whenever you feel a few quarts low on happy.
- **Laugh.** Just laugh. You don"t need a reason, or even a trigger. At any given moment, no matter where you are or what you"re doing, just start laughing. Laughter can give you an instant mood boost that lingers for long periods of time and strengthens your resolve to be happy.

Bee-have

"Trust men and they will be true to you; treat them greatly, and they will show themselves great."
- Ralph Waldo Emerson

The way you treat other people is a reflection of your own attitude. You cannot expect to sustain a positive attitude by acting negatively toward others. Even if your positive mood is not returned, you must strive to retain a sense of dignity and enthusiasm. Eventually, those who begrudge your happiness will either give in and join you, or give up and go away- and in either case, you will be rid of the negative influence without stooping to negativity yourself.

How can you refrain from treating other people poorly? The answer lies in your own behavior. It is not so much what you should do as what you should not do when dealing with negative emotions from others.

Following are some basic guidelines for behaving better and retaining your positive attitude:

DON'T Throw Fits. Many people resort to temper tantrums when they don't get their own way. Some do this without even realizing it. Ranting about the unfairness of the situation will not change things; all it *will* do is generate more negative emotions and fuel the flames. The person you're confronting probably won't give in because you're whining.

Learn to recognize the signs when you start to experience a meltdown, and force yourself to step back and take a more rational look at the situation. There may be more to it than you first noticed.

DON'T Stay Angry. Getting angry is acceptable, and even beneficial in some circumstances. Anger can be a powerful motivating force. However, getting angry is far different from staying angry. Holding on to your anger is counterproductive; you will simply remain where you are in the situation and nothing will change except the level of your anger. When someone or something makes you mad, take that anger and channel its energies into doing something about the situation. If there is nothing to be done, use your anger to do something for yourself. But whatever you do, don't allow anger to keep you rooted to the spot.

DON'T Hold Grudges. Nearly everyone can think of at least one person they have vowed never to speak to again for as long as they live. You may be able to think of several people who fall into this category. Holding a grudge against someone can occur spontaneously, or it can be a carefully planned and executed assault. Some people have elevated grudge-holding to an art form, forcing everyone else around them to take extra precautions with the seating arrangements at family gatherings to avoid putting together people who are loudly ignoring each other. It is easy to form a grudge, and infinitely harder to let one go. However, you must let go of grudges in order to maintain a positive attitude. Maintaining negative feelings for a sustained length of time will taint your mental garden, and provide an automatic supply of negativity whenever you are reminded of the person you"re not speaking to. By nursing a grudge, you are expending energy that could otherwise be used to enrich your own life. If you would rather not speak to whomever it is that angered you, that is a choice you can make. The better choice is to simply agree to disagree, and go your separate ways. Letting go makes you a better person, inside and out.

DON'T Act Superior. Believing you are better than others is a damaging attitude, even when it"s the truth. A little humility goes a long way. When others feel comfortable talking with you, you will find your confidence growing and your attitude improving. Putting someone else down in order to make yourself feel better is a dangerous proposition, and more often than not it will backfire and return to haunt you. Be the best person you can be, but don"t allow yourself to feel superior. We are all only human in the end.

DO Unto Others. The Golden Rule is still the best rule to follow. Treat other people the way you want to be treated, and eventually they will follow your example. When you extend courtesy and kindness to others, it will always come back to you in one form or another, sometimes when you least expect it. Angry words and hurtful action can be forgiven and forgotten, but good deeds linger for a lifetime. Even if the people you treat with respect do not offer the same to you, take comfort in the knowledge that you are behaving with dignity and have nothing to be ashamed of. A lack of shame breeds fearlessness, and those who are fearless can accomplish anything.

Bee flexible

"If we listened to our intellect, we'd never have a love affair. We'd never have a friendship. We'd never go into business, because we'd be too cynical. Well, that's nonsense. You've got to jump off cliffs all the time and build your wings on the way down."
- Ray Bradbury

When life affects your attitude, you must be willing to bend and ready to seek out an alternative path to positivism. Living an inflexible life is akin to standing in the middle of a hurricane. No matter what you choose to hold onto, you will be blown away, and your plans will be changed for you. You must be willing to alter your methods and rules, and allow life to lead you to the places you are intended to go.

We must be willing to adapt to our circumstances if we expect to develop as a person. Eminent evolutionist Charles Darwin once said, "It is not the strongest or most intelligent of the species which survive, but those most adaptable to change." Inflexible structures, no matter how solidly they are built, are more susceptible to breaking. You must learn to bend and give.

Flexibility also allows you to discover new opportunities you might otherwise have missed. For example, you might always drive the same route to work. However, what would you do if the morning traffic report indicated congestion on your usual route? You have a choice: you can either follow the same path you always take and sit in traffic for an extended period of time, or you can choose an alternate route. If you choose an alternate route, you might discover a new restaurant you didn't know was around, or witness a sunrise over a whole new setting.

There are steps you can take to increase your flexibility and prepare yourself to be receptive to change. Here are a few tips to maintaining flexibility and being ready to take advantage of new opportunities as they arise:

- *Give yourself time.* If you are scheduling an appointment or planning to travel somewhere, be sure you have more than enough time to make it. Try to leave a window open: rather than saying "I"ll be there at 7:30," give yourself permission to say "I"ll be there between 7 and 8."
- *Formulate Plan B.* Always have a backup plan ready in case something goes wrong. This way you are not caught unprepared and will have more of an idea what you can do in the absence of your original intentions. It is easier to be flexible when you already have alternatives in mind.
- *Do something different.* If there are certain routines you follow for certain things, try throwing in a few alterations. For example, if you ride public transportation to work and always sit in the same section of the train or bus, decide to sit elsewhere for a few trips. You may notice things you hadn't noticed before, or have the opportunity to meet new people.
- *Be spontaneous.* Whenever possible, do something you would not ordinarily have done. Spontaneity is an excellent way to generate flexibility, because even you

don't know what to expect from yourself, and you will be

forced to

compensate for your lack of planning. Practice improvisation often, and look for creative approaches to typical problems. Different is good, particularly if it allows you to increase your flexibility and capacity for adaption.

Your attitude determines your ultimate outcome. When you develop the ability to control your attitude, you can manufacture your own happiness. Nothing happens without attitude, and the way you feel about anything you do will affect the way it is done.

If you cannot generate a positive attitude right away, you can simply "fake it until you make it." Use the power of positive thinking to convince yourself of your enthusiasm, and soon you will actually begin to feel good about whatever it is you"re trying to accomplish. Life is what you make of it, and your attitude is your life. Tend to it well.

FRUITION AND HARVEST

"There is more to us than we know. If we can be made to see it, perhaps for the rest of our lives we will be unwilling to settle for less."
- Kurt Hahn

The benefits of positive thinking are truly incredible. They can extend to every area of your life, and you will feel like a whole new person. The power of positive thinking is the power of transformation. When you think positively, the changes do not only occur within yourself. The rest of the world will respond to your new outlook as you radiate happiness and pleasant emotions. You will become not only a better person; you will also be a better person to be around.

A good harvest bears good fruit.

Harvesting the fruits of your labor is the most exciting portion of your journey through positive thinking. In this section we will explore the many benefits you can expect to gain through applying positive thinking to all aspects of your life. Once you practice the previously outlined techniques, you will notice that good things seem to just happen to you. You will become the fortunate person you have always envied, the one who seems to be a magnet for love and luck.

Natural Attraction: Bringing Love, Money and Success

"Those who bring sunshine into the lives of others, cannot keep it from themselves."
- Sir James M. Barrie

The power of positive thinking opens up a whole new realm of possibilities. You will discover the effects of maintaining positive thought seeping into all the areas of your life like water absorbed by a sponge. Nothing will remain unchanged as your newfound outlook and attitudes infect your mind, your surroundings and your family and friends with happiness and bring you success beyond your wildest dreams.

Following are just a few of the multitude of benefits positive thinking will bring to your life.

Radiant Relationships

***"A man travels the world over in search of what he needs, and returns home to find it."
- George Moore***

Relationships are essential to our humanity; both our relationships to others and to ourselves. Our relationships define and accentuate who we are, and our ability to relate to others is directly proportional to the manner in which we relate to ourselves. Utilizing positive thinking in our relationships allows us to experience them to the fullest capacity and become infused with love and compassion.

Positive thinking expands, improves and strengthens our relationships. It also allows us to create new relationships and reap the benefits of involvement with others without allowing negativity to taint our lives. Some of the ways positive thinking benefits relationships are:

- Increased trust: In positive thinking, one of the negative practices you will be dismissing is the tendency to lie to yourself. This will automatically quell your tendency to lie to others. When you put forth trust, you receive trust in return;

when you trust yourself, those who care about you will place their trust in you as well.

- Fewer arguments: You will find that your arguments lessen in both frequency and intensity as you progress with positive thinking. Generally, this is because not so many things will bother you, and you will be able to practice forgiveness more often. If you argue frequently with your spouse, your children, other family members or close friends, look forward to a sharp decrease in yelling when you practice positive thinking.

- Improved communication: When you understand yourself, your goals and your priorities, you will be able to articulate your desires more fully. This will lead to better communication, which is the key to any successful relationship. By clearly stating what you are trying to get across, you will automatically encourage others to be straightforward and clear-thinking as well. Your new ability to describe your feelings and motivations may even surprise yourself!

- More understanding: This benefit builds on improved communication. When you are able to explain why you agree or disagree with a certain issue, it will be easier to convince others regarding your point of view- or at least help them see why you are entitled to your opinions. Understanding promotes stronger bonds and less friction in a relationship, and allows both sides of the equation to relax.

- Better sex: Yes, really. The use of positive thinking awakens all of your sensations, including physical pleasure. Applying positive thinking to your relationships can heighten your sex life, in part because you will feel- and therefore be- more attractive. Beauty truly comes from within, and the transformative power of positive thinking will make you more desirable than a swimsuit model.

- Stronger bonds: Positive thinking brings you closer to humanity. You will develop a powerful sense of empathy that will allow you to see things from alternative points of view, including the eyes of other people. Empathy not only lets you forgive mistakes; it also makes you a better friend and confidante: the type of person everyone loves to be around. You will soon discover that there is plenty of you to go around.

- Less stress: Relationships can take a toll on us. It is often quite a strain to keep relationships alive; you must invest time and energy in cultivating and maintaining each one of them. However, the power of positive thinking not only frees you to unburden yourself of unhealthy relationships; it also allows you to be yourself under any circumstances, which lessens the typical strain most of us experience with relationships.

Incredible Careers

"Work is not man's punishment. It is his reward and his strength and his pleasure."
- George Sand

If you believe what the majority of us do, you may think that most people don"t enjoy their jobs. However, the truth is that many people do; they have just forgotten. Many people begin a career with enthusiasm and anticipation, only to discover down the road that their dreams have been crushed by corporate rules.

Positive thinking allows you to wring enjoyment from your career, whether you"re a housewife or a CEO. It is a simple matter to rediscover the reason you entered your chosen career in the first place, and then augment those reasons in your daily work life.

Additionally, many people who choose to seek out the power of positive thinking find out the career they have is not the career they want, no matter how much silver lining they drape around their clouds. Once again, positive thinking steps in to lift you up and settle you into your place in the world.

Here are just a few of the ways positive thinking can benefit your career:

- Recognition: When you practice positive thinking, you become more vibrant and alive than you have ever been. You will find that your efforts are recognized and rewarded more often, particularly when you are not expecting recognition. Simply performing your work with a positive attitude to the best of your abilities will make you stand out.
- Promotions and Raises: Those with can-do attitudes advance far faster in the workplace. Using the power of positive thinking increases your confidence and

demonstrates your capabilities to handle greater responsibility; and those above you at work will notice and treat you accordingly. You will not only be offered more opportunity; you will find yourself seeking advancement and fulfillment rather than simply waiting for the day to end so you can return to your "real" life. Your career will become a part of what defines you instead of a means of survival that you just "get through."

- Better Working Environment: You may recall that positive thinking is contagious. Working with a pleasant attitude will improve the attitudes of those around you, or at least your perceptions of them. You will begin to notice that your workday no longer drags you down as you derive pleasure from your accomplishments and enjoy the company of your co-workers.

- Less Supervision: Most of us know what it"s like to have a supervisor breathing down our necks. When we move to a positive mindset, we showcase our abilities to complete work satisfactorily without excessive direction (or interference). Left to our own devices, we will accomplish far more- and this will become evident to even the most anal of supervisors.

- Dream Job: With positive thinking, you can live your dreams. Whether you choose to seek a new career or transform the job you have into the job you love, you will soon find your career providing everything you imagine it to be.

- Entrepreneurship: Many people long to go into business for themselves, but most fear the consequences of losing the safety and security of working for someone else. Positive thinking frees you from your fear of change, and equips you with the tools you need to not only take steps toward working for yourself, but carry your entrepreneurial vision to success. Whatever your reasons for wanting your own business, you can use positive thinking to bypass the pitfalls that plague most beginning business ventures and realize your dreams of self-employment.

- New opportunities: Positive thinking allows you to visualize possibilities you would have otherwise missed. As you get to know yourself, your beliefs and your desires; you will better understand what you"re looking for in a career. You will also have the ability to discover the means to achieve what you want, whether it is improving your current job, getting a promotion or new position, or heading off on your own. There is no limit to the opportunities awaiting you through the power of positive thinking.

Financial Freedom

> *"If a person gets his attitude toward money straight, it will help straighten out almost every other area in his life."*
> *- Billy Graham*

This is not to say positive thinking will make you rich, though that is a distinct possibility. Achieving financial freedom is releasing yourself from the worries money brings and allowing yourself to always have enough, if not an abundance.

Some of the ways positive thinking promotes financial freedom:

- **Unlimited possibilities.** When you realize that any avenue is open to you, you can take steps toward setting and reaching your financial goals, whether you want to be comfortable and debt-free or living in an ocean-side mansion.

- **Productive work environment.** Because positive thinking equips you with the capacity to truly enjoy your job, you will find yourself performing far better and automatically earning more, whether it"s in the form of raises, promotions, or the decision that you are better off somewhere else.

- **Lower cash outflow.** As you practice positive thinking techniques, you will find yourself spending less money. Because you are responsible and confident, there will be fewer emergencies and disasters in your life, and misfortune will become a rare happenstance; a mere memory. Spending less to gain more is one of the many long-term benefits of positive thinking. You will also find that you need fewer material objects to satisfy yourself as you become richer in spirit.

Dream Delivery

"If you have built castles in the air, your work need not be lost; there is where they belong. Now put foundations under them."
- Henry David Thoreau

Whatever your dreams are for your life, positive thinking can help you achieve them. Lifelong dreams can take many forms, whether it is traveling to an exotic place, performing a daredevil stunt, or meeting a particular celebrity. With positive thinking, you can take the necessary steps to make your fondest dreams a reality.

It"s said that a goal is a dream with a deadline. Positive thinking helps you realize not only that you can live your dreams, but that you deserve to live them. Positive thinking allows you to:

- Understand that no dream is too great or too small.
- Develop a mindset that is conducive to dream fulfillment.
- Formulate a concrete, manageable plan for making your dreams come true.
- Equip yourself with the determination necessary to keep going until you reach your dream.

- Dream bigger than you ever would have, with the realization that there is no limit to what you can accomplish.

Awesome Aging

***"Youth is a circumstance you can't do anything about. The trick is to grow up without getting old."
- Frank Lloyd Wright***

What"s so great about aging? Everything, when you view it through the lens of positive thinking. Applying positive thinking methods to the aging process produces incredible effect: studies have proven that happy people live, on average, 7.5 years longer than unhappy people- a better advantage than not smoking, exercising regularly, and maintaining a healthy weight combined.

By allowing yourself to view aging as an experience rather than an ordeal, you give yourself the gift of time. Here are some other benefits of a positive outlook on aging:

- *Lowered blood pressure and reduced cholesterol.* Happy people don"t experience much stress. They also tend to keep themselves in better shape. Some researchers attribute the increase in life span among positive people to the corresponding decrease in blood pressure and cholesterol.

- *Stronger will to live.* As we age, many of us tend to lapse into a depressive state. We often reflect on our lives and decide we have done nothing to merit worth, and it is then we begin to die. With positive thinking, we can realize that it is never too late to do something with ourselves and our lives; that all is not lost.

- *Preservation of independence.* You may notice that some older people seem far younger and more able than others their age. The major difference between a 70-year-old who lives at home, stays busy, and maintains an active family life; and a 70-year-old who is inactive and consigned to a wheelchair in a nursing home; is attitude. The senior at home believes it is possible to live a healthy, happy life no matter how old they get, while the senior in the home believes there is nothing to look forward to.

THE PHYSICAL POWER OF POSITIVE THINKING

"Take care of your body with steadfast fidelity. The soul must see through these eyes alone, and if they are dim, the whole world is clouded."
- Goethe

You know that positive thinking improves your mental health. But did you know It can also improve your physical health? The power of your thoughts is so strong, it can actually affect the way your body behaves and improve a host of physical ailments- or even bring you from the brink of death.

Take Christopher Reeve. The actor who will be forever remembered for his powerful performance as Superman will also be remembered for his remarkable recovery after a horse-riding accident left him completely paralyzed. Yet not only did Reeve live far longer than any doctor predicted, he made great strides toward recovery and was able to move parts of his body that were pronounced forever lost to him before his death in 2004. Reeve survived for nine years after the accident and proved he truly was a super man.

How did he do it? Positive thinking. According to researchers who analyzed his case, Reeve"s optimistic attitude and can-do mindset were almost entirely responsible for the unparalleled level of recovery he experienced.

When you banish negative thoughts from your mind, your physical health responds tremendously. It has long been known that there is a correlation between emotional and physical health; often referred to as the "mind-body connection." Improving your outlook and practicing positive thinking strengthens your mind-body connection and makes you healthy, even to the point of extending your life.

Studies have shown that depression and negative thought decreases antibodies and leaves you more open to infection and disease. Those who are unhappy or stressed exhibit weaker immune responses to vaccines; take longer to heal; are more susceptible to colds and viruses; and experience stronger symptoms.

There is documented scientific evidence that electrical activity in the brain related to emotion has a direct effect on the body"s ability to heal and fights off disease. Negative thoughts produce a surge of activity in the right prefrontal cortex, which brings about a weak immune response; while positive thoughts produce activity in the left prefrontal cortex and strengthens immune response. It is true: happy people are healthier, simply because they are happy!

A positive thought program may also possess the ability to protect you from Alzheimer"s or other degenerative aging diseases. Because part of the process of positive thinking involves a continual quest for self-improvement and encourages you to stay mentally active, your mind will be in better shape as you age and you will be less susceptible to degenerative disease such as Alzheimer"s, osteoporosis and rheumatoid arthritis. A sharp mind helps to maintain a sharp body.

Don"t underestimate the power of positive thinking in regards to your own health. You *can* think yourself healthy; and you will find that you have more energy, fewer colds, and an increased vitality. Perhaps some day, science will discover a way to inject happiness as a means to combat disease. Until then, we will have to be responsible for creating our own happiness.

Sit Back and Relax

"It is time to break through the barriers that have held you back and held you down for such a long time. It is time to reach out and indelibly etch your place in history."
- Greg Hickman

Are you ready for a new life?

Positive thinking arms you with all the tools you need to achieve your deepest hopes, wishes and desires. You will be equipped to deal with any of the circumstances life presents you with, and receptive to the boundless possibilities that come with true happiness. Once you have planted and tended your mental garden, you can sit back and enjoy the harvest of success.

When you reach fruition of your positive thinking goals, it is important to relax and enjoy your accomplishments. You will not be motivated to move further in your life if you do not take the time to experience the benefits of all your hard work. Many people don't know how to relax, and simply continue to push themselves believing that eventually, relaxation and reward will come to them. This is not the case: you must take the time for yourself to reap what you have sown in your mental garden.

Following are several suggestions to help you take in the true measure of your successes and use them to further even more positive gain:

- **Take a "me" day.** When you have reached a major goal, take an entire day for yourself. You"ve earned it. Engage in your favorite activities: read a good book, watch a movie, dine at your favorite restaurant. Pamper yourself: take a long bath, buy yourself a decadent dessert, get a professional massage. Refuse to do favors for anyone else on this day. Tell others that you are celebrating your success and indulge in good feelings. You will feel wonderful, and you will cement your achievements in your mind. Awareness of your progress is integral to your continued success.
- **Spread the joy.** Do you know someone with similar goals and ambitions? Take the time to share your accomplishments with anyone you feel will benefit from them. Tell them how you achieved your goals and share the

secrets of your success. Changing your own life produces a powerful feeling, and when you use your own transformation to help others change as well, your own benefits are amplified. Happiness and success cannot be contained and kept for ourselves. Facilitate the spread of joy whenever possible, and you will find your efforts circling back to you again and again.

- **Count your blessings.** The more you accomplish, the more you stand to accomplish. Reflecting on the full realization of the completion of your goals will help you solidify your positive mindset. There may be benefits to your achievements that you have yet to realize. What have you gained by reaching your goals? Create a mental catalogue of all the ways your life is enriched by positive thinking and refer to it often. This practice adds to your arsenal of empowerment tools and exponentially increases your capacity to gain.

- **Preserve the lesson.** Just as you kept a journal of your progress toward the completion of your goals, you should keep a written record of your successes. The ability to reflect on change and the steps that led to it is crucial to your continued advancement. You may find yourself facing a similar challenge in the future, and having a set of written records to refer to saves you the mental difficulties of going through the process all over again as though you had never done it before. Additionally, writing down what you have learned enables you to discover the deeper meaning of all you have achieved, and everything you have gained in excess of your main objective.

- **Start over.** The sentiment "quit while you"re ahead" has no place in positive thinking. Though it is necessary to enjoy the rewards of your labor, it is equally necessary to set new goals; aim for higher standards. Never cease to learn and grow. When you have reached a point in your life that you feel satisfies your wishes and dreams, create new wishes and manufacture more dreams. Life is not a destination; it is a journey. To achieve perfection is to settle for complacency and stop living. We begin to die the moment we cease to change.

Enjoy the good things that flow from success.

Relax! You've earned it. Just don't forget to continue your quest for a fulfilled life after each success. Use positive thinking to accomplish any goal, whether it is organizing your desk or traveling the world. You can achieve your dreams, and you can start today. The best time to begin your journey toward fulfillment is *right now*.

CONCLUSION

"The bad news is time flies. The good news is you're the pilot."
- Michael Althsuler

Surviving the Winter: Keep Your Garden Alive

Now that you have enjoyed the harvest of your flourishing mental garden, you must ensure that you will continue to produce a new crop, year after year. You cannot stop the rain from falling- but you can choose how you view it when it comes. You cannot avoid the passage of time and its eroding effects- but you can teach yourself to recognize when it is time to replant. You cannot keep others out of your garden- but you can choose to let them in.

With practice you will learn to weather the hard times and emerge from hibernation stronger each time. The more you use positive thinking, the greater your mental strength will become. You are firmly on the path to achieving what you desire from life, and the longer you remain, the more difficult it will be for anything to deter you.

*"He who chooses the beginning of a road chooses the place it leads to.
It is the means that determines the end."
- Harry Emerson Fosdick*

Your journey has begun. Where it ends is entirely up to you.

CHECKLIST FOR THE POSITIVE THINKING PROCESS

When you begin a project or engage in self-improvement, follow these steps to tap in to the power of positive thinking.

- Banish negative thoughts from your mind.
- Decide to accomplish your goal.
- Formulate a set of positive thoughts revolving around your goal.
- Develop a step-by-step plan to reach your goal.
- Keep a journal of your thoughts and your progress.
- Practice getting out of your own way.
- Be flexible and prepared to start over in the event of setbacks.
- Visualize yourself achieving your goal.
- Maintain a positive attitude toward your goal.
- Do not allow the opinions of others to deter you from your path.
- Engage in daily self-confidence exercises to keep your goal fresh.
- Be yourself, behave, and be happy.
- Recognize when you have reached your goal and enjoy your success.

- Reflect on the path that has brought you to your goal.
- Record your reactions and feedback for future reference.

BIBLIOGRAPHY

Beaulac, Andrew. "Yak Riders on Meditation Methods." http://www.yakrider.com/meditation_methods.htm, January 2000

Brescia, Michael. *Today is Your Day to Win.* New York: Michael Brescia 2000

Chiles, James R. *Inviting Disaster: Tales from the Edge of Technology.* New York: HarperCollins Publishers, Inc., 2001, 2002

Hansard, Christopher. *The Tibetan Art of Positive Thinking: Skillful Thoughts for Successful Living.* New York: Atria, August 2005

Peale, Norman Vincent. *The Power of Positive Thinking.* New York: Random House, Inc., 1952

"Power of a super attitude: Reeve"s life bolsters theories on mind-body health link." *USA Today*: Sharon Jayson, October 13, 2004, p. 6D

www.ingramcontent.com/pod-product-compliance
Lightning Source LLC
Chambersburg PA
CBHW060459010526
44118CB00018B/2473